HOW I FOUND MY PARADISE

....AND SO, CAN YOU

MYRIAM GRAJALES

Purposeful Pages Press
ISBN 979-8-9998704-1-4

I dedicate this book with all my love to my children. Bryan, Michael, Karen and Jessica, because with each one I have learned to grow, to my siblings who have always been there for me, and to all the people who have passed through my life because everyone has left a lesson.
Thank you, thank you, thank you I also dedicate this book to my past self, for not giving up. To my present self, for daring.
To my future self, to keep dreaming.

DEDICATION TO READERS:

To you, who look for your own light in the middle of the fog. This book is a map, but you are the way.
And to all the brave souls who hit rock bottom and decided to build their heaven from there.

TABLE OF CONTENTS

PROLOGUE 5
CHAPTER 1 8
MY HELL 8
CHAPTER 2 22
FORGIVENESS 22
CHAPTER 3 29
KNOW YOURSELF 29
CHAPTER 4 35
STRENGTHEN YOUR SELF-ESTEEM 35
CHAPTER 5 47
ASSUME RESPONSIBILITY 47
CHAPTER 6 52
GRATITUDE 52
EMPATHY AND COMPASSION 57
CHAPTER 8 63
FEAR 63
.... 67
CHAPTER 9 68
PROCRASTINATION 68
CHAPTER 10 73
INTERNAL DIALOGUE 73
CHAPTER 11 80
The Power of Choice 80
CHAPTER 12 86
THE POWER OF THE PRESENT 86
CHAPTER 13 90
IMPORTANCE OF HEALTHY BOUNDARIES 90
CHAPTER 14 96
INSOMNIA 96

CHAPTER 15 108
GOODBYE TO CIGARETTES, HELLO TO YOU 108

CHAPTER 16 124
FREE YOURSELF FROM EXCESS WEIGHT 124

CHAPTER 17 133
FREEING YOU FROM PHOBIAS 133

CHAPTER 18 145
CHANGING NEGATIVE THOUGHTS 146

CHAPTER 19 153
HOW TO IMPROVE YOUR MEMORY 153

HEALING THE RELATIONSHIP WITH ALCOHOL 160

CHAPTER 21 169
ACT AS IF YOU HAD ALREADY FOUND PARADISE
.... 169

CLOSING MESSAGE 174

MESSAGE TO THE READER 176

TESTIMONIALS FROM THERAPIES WITH MYRIAM GRAJALES 177

BIOGRAPHY 183

PROLOGUE

This book was born from a deep desire to heal… and to help others heal. It is not made of theory or pretty phrases, but of real life: of open wounds, of dark memories, and of the light that I found when I chose to let go of the past. I lived trapped in hell for many years. A hell that began in my childhood, marked by sexual, physical, and emotional abuse. I survived fear, hate, guilt, and a sadness so deep that, at times, I wanted to disappear. But there was a day that marked the beginning of my rebirth.

That day, guided by a hypnotherapy of forgiveness, I went down to the deepest place of my soul... and there, I understood that the only way out was to let go of hatred. **Forgive.** Not for others, but for me. It was like a giant stone fell from my back.

For the first time in decades, I could breathe. I could see the sky, the flowers, life. And I knew that **it was possible to heal.**

Since then, an inner journey began that changed my existence: I rediscovered myself, my power and my purpose. And I decided to become a hypnotherapist to share this path with others.

This book is not just my story. It is a guide for those who feel like they are broken inside, for those who believe there is no way out. It is an extended hand so you know that you too can heal. Your paradise is not far away; **it is within you.**

Thanks for being here.

If this book has come into your hands, it is no coincidence. It's your soul telling you that it's time to free yourself.

With love, **Myriam Grajales**

CHAPTER 1

MY HELL

This chapter is not intended to provoke pity but to show you the exact point from where my journey began. Here my story begins... from the hell where I was born. Not all childhoods begin with fairy tales. Some begin with fear, with blows, with silences that hurt more than words. Mine was like this.

I was a girl surrounded by screams, deprivation, and violence. I lived in a house where danger did not come from outside but slept under the same roof. Where learning to hide was more important than learning to play.

I grew up believing that this was normal. That parents were like that. That pain was part of being a daughter. I got used to being silent. I got used to not expecting anything. I became a sad, shy girl who looked at the world from an open wound.

In the midst of that darkness, there was a woman who gave me something similar to light: my mother.

She was loving and protective to the extent that fear would allow. But she lived in fear. Terrified of her husband, of his reactions, of his unpredictable violence.

I saw her many times with her gaze lost, with her body bruised and her soul worn out. Even so, she never stopped fighting for us.

My father, on the other hand, was the shadow that covered everything. An alcoholic man, emotionally absent, present only to spread terror. He spent his days lying in bed, reading cowboy novels, while my mother made a living raising chickens and selling eggs to feed seven children. But every night, he would take her hard-earned money... return drunk, and hell would begin again.

I was the second of seven siblings. Life at home was hard, very hard. Poverty was constant, but the real pain did not come from the lack of material things but from the violence that was breathed out daily.

And amid all that, **my childhood was stolen.**

My father not only sexually abused me since I was a little girl, but he also beat me with leather whips; he constantly insulted me. He told me that I was stupid and useless and that I would never amount to anything in life.

And of course, I believed it.

Because when you are a child, you believe that your parents have the truth in their mouths.

And if they say you're worthless... you swallow it as if it were the law.

His violence was constant. His abuse, repeated. He looked for any moment of inattention, any excuse to get closer, to impose himself. It was like living in a cell without bars: no one saw it, no one knew it, but I had nowhere to run.

This continued until I was fifteen. Fifteen years trapped in the body of a used, beaten, confused girl. Until one day, hell opened, but for him.

He was abusing me once again... and my aunt discovered us. I remember her scream, her fury. I remember how she lunged at him, and they started hitting each other.

My sisters ran to look for my mother, who was working. His father's family also intervened.

And finally, they kicked him out of the house. I don't know where he went. Disappeared. And with his departure, for the first time, a little air entered our lives.

After my father left, my mother was left alone with seven children and a past full of wounds, but also with a strength that only women who have survived fear have.

That woman, the same one who had lived for years with terror in her body, stood up like never before.

With patience, effort, and a tireless spirit, she began to build our future. Little by little, with the little she had, she started her first business. She raised chickens and hens, sold them and saved every coin as if it were gold. And one day, with that constant saving and her unwavering determination, she managed to buy a bigger house. For us, it was a castle. A miracle. A home where we could finally breathe.

I remember how she said,

"From grain to grain, the hen fills the crop."

She repeated that phrase like a mantra, and today I understand that it was more than an expression: it was her philosophy of life.

Years later, she opened not one, but two more coffee shops. She handled them with admirable intelligence, although she had only studied up to third grade. She did calculations by heart, she did the accounting in her head, she took percentages and she knew how to manage costs and employees. She was a wise woman without titles, a natural psychologist who treated her workers with respect and compassion. I don't know where she got so much from, but today I can say that she was one of my greatest teachers.

Thanks to her efforts, we were able to study.

She told us that it was more important to give us education than money, because with education we could make our way. And so, she did: **she gave us wings.**

However, although my surroundings began to improve, the remains of hell still lived within me.

The issue of abuse was never raised again. Maybe because of shame. Maybe because of pain. Maybe because of guilt... although she wasn't guilty. She had also been a victim.

My father had abused her, mistreated her and reduced her. I found out later, and that revelation made me see her with even more love.

But the hatred I felt for him was still alive in me. It was an immense, dark hatred that consumed me inside. To me, he was the devil himself. And back then, I didn't believe in God.

How could there be a God who allowed so much suffering, so much injustice? How could there be a God who watched a girl being abused day after day and did nothing?

I lived through fifteen years of real abuse. And then I lived another fifteen with that hell in my mind. I became an adult trapped in the past, feeling like the unhappiest girl in the world.

I became a victim of my memories, my resentment, my low self- esteem and my depression. Blaming me. Punishing me.

Believing I didn't deserve anything good. Because the abuser also convinces you that you are worthless. And you believe it.

Time passed, and, like many people who have survived trauma, I tried to build a "normal" life. I got married. I had four children: two boys and identical twin girls. I had a good job, a high salary, and a house in a good neighborhood. From the outside, everything seemed fine. But inside, there were still wounds that had never fully healed.

Because of my work responsibilities and because I earned much more than my husband, he took on the household chores and money management. I completely trusted him. I dedicated my little free time to be with my children, taking care of them, giving them what I didn't have.

Until one day, everything collapsed. I found a letter from the bank. A warning. It said that in a month they would foreclose on our house. I didn't understand it. It was almost paid. How was it possible?

I started investigating. I discovered that all our credit cards, with very high limits due to my good financial history, were completely full. All in collection offices. The money was gone.

My world fell apart. I asked my husband what he had done. He didn't say anything. He locked himself in his silence.

Years later I learned that he had become addicted to gambling. Dog runs. While I worked non-stop, he had destroyed our financial stability. I felt like my life was falling apart.

And with it, everything that had cost me so much to sustain.

I fell into a deep depression. I looked at my children and only thought that I didn't want them to experience what I experienced. But I didn't see a way out. I remember one afternoon... I put my children in the car. I drove to some train tracks. I stood there, waiting for the train to pass. I wanted to die, and I didn't want to leave my children alone, so I took them with me.

But the train didn't arrive. Time passed. The children began to cry. And then I came home, defeated. I locked myself in the room. I stopped eating, showering and talking. I wanted to let myself die.

My husband called the doctor. He understood the gravity and told him to take me by force if necessary.

I ended up under psychiatric treatment. They prescribed me medications that made me feel worse: I heard voices and I became more lost inside myself. I also had psychological therapy, but nothing worked.

The psychologist told me, "You are going to be here until I decide to speak". But I had no words. Just tears. And the desire to disappear.

Days passed, and I did not improve. That's when she appeared: **my best friend.** The one that didn't leave when everyone disappeared. The one who decided to find another way to help me. She learned about something called hypnotherapy. She didn't really know how it worked, but she found a therapist about an hour away. She paid for the sessions because I had no money. She took me there. And without knowing it, **she was saving my life.**

I didn't know what to expect from hypnotherapy. At that moment, nothing made sense to me. I just knew I was broken, empty. desperate.

During the first session, the therapist spoke softly to me. He explained that he would guide me to my subconscious, the place where the true roots of my suffering were.

It wasn't magic, nor a trick. **It was a journey inward.** To where everything had started. And there, in the depths of my mind, memories that I had buried for years began to emerge. Images, sensations, emotions. I saw my father. I saw that girl who had been me. Scared. Quiet. Alone. I revived the hate. The fear. The hopelessness.

And I understood something that I had never been able to see clearly: my whole life revolved around hate. It was like my world was built on that emotion.

The hatred I had for my father was so great, so deep, that it had gotten into every part of me: in my body, in my mind, in my decisions, in my health, and in my spirit.

I couldn't move forward because I was chained to him.

And then, the therapist took me to a place I had never imagined: **forgiveness.** At first, the word alone turned me upside down. Forgive him? The man who had destroyed my childhood?

But the therapist didn't tell me to forgive him for him. He showed me that forgiveness was not for justifying. **It was to free me.** And it was there, at that moment, that something inside me broke... or rather, let go.

I felt like a huge stone fell from my back. As if for the first time in my life I could really breathe. I left that session and saw everything differently. The sky was bluer. The most vivid flowers. The air had a different flavor. It was as if my soul had been locked away... and a door had finally opened.

The depression didn't go away immediately, but it no longer had the same strength. Now I knew I wasn't broken. I was hurt, yes. But I could heal.

However, external problems were still there. The bank's process to take possession of my house continued. The collectors didn't stop. And I knew that if I didn't put distance, I could fall again. So, I made a difficult but necessary decision:

I went with my children to Colombia. Returning to Colombia was an act of survival.

It was not a planned trip, nor a pleasant getaway. It was the only way out I found to avoid falling into the abyss again. I took my children with me.

All I wanted was a little silence. Get away from the calls, the letters, and the debt collectors who didn't let me breathe.

And there, in Colombia, I came face to face with him: my father. The man I had hated my entire life. The man who was my hell. But he was no longer the same. He was sick. Very sick. Cirrhosis, a consequence of so many years of alcohol, had weakened him until it left his skin stuck to his bones. He could barely breathe. He depended on an oxygen tank.

And I, who had promised never to forgive him, found myself... caring for him. For a whole year I was by his side. Taking care of him. Feeding him. Watching life slowly escape from his body.

And the most surprising thing is that I didn't do it with resentment. I did it with compassion. I no longer felt hatred. I didn't remember his violence when I saw him so fragile. His presence didn't hurt me. What hurt me was his abandonment of himself. His illness. His loneliness. I took care of him with love. As if my soul had changed its skin.

One day, while I was helping him in his bed, I said to him in a calm voice, "Daddy... if you regret all the damage that you did and ask for forgiveness, you will be able to rest." He looked at me and responded with a weak voice, "Daughter... I don't have to apologize. I have never done harm to anyone."

I was speechless. That moment was a revelation.

He wasn't going to change. He was never going to acknowledge the damage. And yet, I had already forgiven him.

Because I understood that forgiveness does not depend on the other person. It depends on me. Waiting for the other person to accept their guilt is to remain tied. To forgive is to cut that rope.

I understood that the hatred I carried for so long was like drinking poison every day... hoping it would hurt him. But I was taking the poison myself.

I returned to the United States with a different soul. I had lovingly cared for the man who hurt me so much. And that **set me free.**

When I returned to the United States, I was no longer the same.

He had gone through the fire. I had taken care of the one who had been my greatest pain. And I didn't break. On the contrary, something inside me ordered itself.

I felt a deep need to understand what had happened. How was it possible that after so much hatred, I had cared for him with love? What had changed in me?

I looked for answers where I felt they might be: the mind. I immersed myself in books, in studies, and in questions. One of the first that came into my hands was Many Lives, Many Masters, by Brian Weiss. And there, everything clicked.

I understood that hypnotherapy had not only saved my life... I woke up.

I realized I wanted to do the same for others. That just as my friend extended her hand to me when I couldn't do it alone, I wanted to extend it now to those who are still trapped in their own hell, believing that there is no way out. I decided to heal all my fears.

One by one. Look at them straight. Breathe them. Release them. It was like stepping out of an emotional garbage dump, full of darkness, and walking into a garden full of light.

It was like removing chains that I had worn all my life without realizing it.

And then, I knew:
This was my purpose.
I studied hypnotherapy. I trained. I transformed.

And now, from the other side of the tunnel, I write these pages for you.
Because if I could get out of hell...
You can too.
Because if I found my paradise, you can find yours too.

CHAPTER 2

FORGIVENESS

Anger is not the same as hate. Anger is an automatic and fleeting emotion. It arises in the moment, explodes, and, if allowed, dissolves.

Hate, on the other hand, is a deeper choice: it feeds on memory, stays alive with thought, and becomes an emotional prison.

Persisting in remembering what hurts us prevents the wounds from healing. It robs us of the ability to fully live in the present.

There are different types of hate: On the one hand, there is rational or justified hatred, such as that born of abuse, betrayal, or injustice. On the other hand, there are irrational hatreds, such as racism or fanaticism. But all of them, without exception, have something in common: they are the opposite of love... and freedom.

Hate is a burden that we carry day after day. But it does not punish those who hurt us... It punishes us. It steals our peace, sleep, and joy. It keeps us chained to the person we most want to forget.

I know it very well. I lived fifteen years hating my father while he raped me. And then I lived another fifteen years hating him for what he had done to me. Thirty years trapped in my hell. Because yes, hell **exists, but it is in the mind.** Made of memories, pain, and hate.

Holding rancor is like drinking poison hoping it will hurt the other person. But while that person goes on with his life... we get sick. In the soul, in the body, in the mind.

Resentment generates sadness, bitterness, anxiety, and depression. It is a stain that spreads over the soul and gradually extinguishes the light.

Forgiving is not forgetting. Forgiving is not justifying. Forgiveness is freedom.
It is regaining power over our lives.

When we forgive, we stop being victims and become **heroes of our story**. Forgiveness is not a gift for the other person... It is a gift for us. It is choosing to live without chains. It's letting go of the stone.
It's breathing again.

Forgiveness does not mean reconciliation. It does not mean allowing harm again. It means saying, "I **no longer give you my peace.**" It means recognizing that we cannot change the past, but we can change how it affects us today.

Whoever does harm reveals the hell within. We can't control what others do, but we can control how we respond. And that makes all the difference.

When we hate, we relive over and over what they did to us. We get stuck in the past.

And while we do so, we lose the only moment that exists: **the present.**

The desire for revenge does not harm others; it only steals our peace.

Forgiveness is accepting that the hurt occurred, but it does not have to define us. That is to say, "Enough. Up to this point I gave you power over me."

We don't need the other person to repent. We don't need them to apologize. **Our peace is much more important.**

Forgiveness is a process, yes. It's not easy. But it is the first step towards true healing. When we forgive, everything begins to change:

- Our relationships become healthier.
- Our health improves.
- Depression is relieved.
- Blood pressure decreases.
- The immune system is strengthened.

- Self-esteem flourishes.

How to forgive?

Here I share exercises that helped me and that can help you.

Exercise 1: Give yourself the gift of forgiveness.

Make it conscious. Say out loud:

"Today I chose to forgive. I deserve to live free."

Exercise 2: Recognize what you feel.

Identify the hatred or resentment that you carry inside.

Allow yourself to feel it without judging yourself. Cry if you have to.

Recognizing it is the first step to letting go.

Exercise 3: The liberating letter

Take a blank sheet of paper. Write everything you feel towards that person.

Express yourself without filters: pain, anger, and insults if you need them.

Let off steam.

Then go outside, crumple the paper, and burn it. As the smoke rises, say:

"I forgive you and set you free. I forgive myself for having carried this hatred."

Repeat this exercise as many times as you need until you feel light.

Exercise 4: Write a letter of forgiveness.

You don't need to send it. Just express yourself. Tell him that you choose to let go of the resentment.

Release it with words.

Exercise 5: The healing mirror

In front of a mirror, look into your eyes and say:

"(Your name), I forgive you; I love you, and I accept you as you are.

You are a perfect creation."

Then say:

"I forgive myself; I love myself, and I accept myself as I am.

"I am a perfect creation."

Repeat this many times. What we repeat, the subconscious takes as truth.

Forgiving does not change the past.
But it does change your present...and your future.

Forgiveness is not forgetting what happened; it is remembering without it hurting. It's looking back and seeing how much you've grown,
It's letting go of the weight... and starting to fly.

CHAPTER 3

KNOW YOURSELF

After forgiving my father, I understood that it was time to look inward. I had spent so much time carrying hate and pain that I had forgotten who I really was. Thus began my most important journey: the journey towards myself.

I wanted to know my weaknesses, my strengths, and my emotions. I wanted to understand why I reacted the way I did. I wanted to know what I could improve and what I could heal.

I started by writing down on paper all the criticism I had received throughout my life: from family, acquaintances, and even from people who barely knew me. I noticed that some of them repeated themselves: they said I was explosive, angry, and hysterical. And I recognized it. Yes, I was.

It wasn't easy to accept it, but that's where the transformation began. "One day at a time," I repeated to myself.

> **"Just for today I'm going to control my emotions. Just for today I'm going to breathe deeply and master my mind."**

Every new day is a new opportunity.

The power of self-knowledge

Knowing yourself sets you free. When you know yourself, you don't need anyone's approval. You don't care about likes, gossip, or the judgments of others.

You know who you are. And that's enough.

People who are offended by criticism often fear that others know them better than they know themselves. But when you already know yourself, **you have power.**

When you don't react to offenses, you have gained emotional intelligence. Your silence becomes your most powerful response.

Remember:

A criticism is just an opinion. And it only has the weight that you give it.

The energy we spend reacting to others… We can use it to grow, to heal, and to live. Only when we accept and love ourselves can we truly love others. Only when we have peace inside can we share it with those around us.

Accepting yourself is freeing you.

Learn to accept who you are: your lights, your shadows, your wounds, and your gifts. You don't have to prove anything to anyone. Accept what you cannot change, and work with love on what you can transform. One day at a time.

Love starts with you. Warm your heart. Because in a warm heart, sadness or fear does not enter... only love.

Happiness is not outside. It is not in people, places, or things. It is within you. And it only appears when you know yourself, accept yourself, and truly love yourself. Free yourself from beliefs that are not yours. Question what you believe.

Many of our ideas come from our parents, school, culture, and religion. But are they true for you today? Do they serve you in your current life?

Don't be afraid to change what you've learned. Don't cling to what limits you. Get out of the box of beliefs you inherited and create your own truth.

The past cannot be changed. You can only learn from it. And move forward with more awareness. Become your priority.

Your life is yours. And it is limited. Don't waste it trying to please everyone. You are not a gold coin. Not everyone will understand your path. And you don't need them to.

Make decisions that make you happy, even if others don't like them. Do what sets your soul on fire. Learn to say "yes" with enthusiasm and "no" without guilt.

Remember:

"Every time you do something just to please others, you lose a piece of yourself."

Return to Yourself

Spend time with yourself. Connect with nature. Walk barefoot, watch the sunset, and listen to the silence. Enjoy your own company. Do not fear solitude. Solitude is the space where the soul whispers.

Be kind to yourself.

Don't judge yourself.

Don't betray yourself.

Choose every day what brings you peace. Value what *you* think of yourself. Don't live to impress anyone. Do something for yourself every day. And don't search for the meaning of life…

Search for a purpose that ignites you.

Your Greatest Battle is Internal

Your biggest enemy isn't outside. It's within you: it's your mind when you don't know how to control it. It's that thought that sabotages you, that judges you, that makes you doubt.

But you have the power. Every time you face an obstacle, ask yourself:

"Will this destroy me or strengthen me?"

Don't regret your mistakes. Thanks to them, you are who you are today. Thanks to them, you know what you know. They are your teacher.

Never Stop Learning

Always keep a beginner's mindset: open, humble, and curious. Don't be afraid to say, **"I don't know."** Reread the books that marked your path. You'll discover new lessons. Because every time you grow, your perspective changes. And you see everything from a new level.

Become Your Best Version

You don't need to be perfect. You just need to be true to yourself. Work on yourself. For yourself. And because of yourself. Make yourself your priority—without selfishness or guilt. Balance is the key:

Love yourself without forgetting others also matter. Let go of what doesn't nourish you: people, habits, and beliefs. Do it little by little, but do it. And repeat to yourself every day:

Today I choose to know myself, accept myself,

and love myself.

Today I choose to be true to me."

Self Esteem

CHAPTER 4

STRENGTHEN YOUR SELF-ESTEEM

One of the most damaging forms of abuse I experienced in my childhood was emotional abuse. My father used to tell me I was stupid, that I would never achieve anything, and that I was worthless. He constantly mocked me. And I, as a little girl, believed him.

I grew up with shattered self-esteem, with insecurities so deeply rooted they became part of my identity. Since I'm short, any comment about something small felt like a personal attack, and I would explode. I remember one of my brothers-in-law used to make jokes about my height, and it made me furious.

But when I started to love and accept myself just as I am, those comments stopped affecting me. One day I asked him why he didn't joke about my height anymore, and he replied:

"Because it's no longer fun... You don't get upset anymore."

That's when I realized a powerful truth: *when you change on the inside, the world changes with you.*

What destroys self-esteem?

Low self-esteem is often the result of deep wounds: physical, emotional, or sexual abuse; lack of affection in childhood; parenting based on criticism instead of praise; authoritarianism; neglect; bullying; unprocessed failures; or constant comparisons. All of this makes you feel worthless, not enough, and alone.

Sometimes we don't even notice it, but that emptiness shows up in toxic relationships, emotional dependence, fear of speaking up, inability to set boundaries, and constant insecurity.

We tell ourselves terrible things:

"I'm useless."

"Nothing ever works out for me."

"Everyone else is better than me."

And without realizing it, we become our own worst enemy. But the good news is you can change all of that.

How to start healing your self-esteem?

First, remember this: it's not what happened to you that defines you—it's what you do with it. Stop blaming yourself. Stop seeking validation outside yourself. Stop saying things to yourself that you would never say to someone you love.

Starting today, choose to be your own best friend. Your cheerleader. You're a rock.

Because if *you* aren't there for yourself, who will be? Your subconscious mind can't tell the difference between truth and a lie. — it believes what you repeat to it. So, start speaking to yourself with love.

Reprogram your inner dialogue. And when a negative thought shows up, change it immediately. Instead of saying, "I can't," say, "I'm learning." Instead of "I'm a mess," say, "I'm building myself with patience."

Exercise 1: Heal your inner child

Find a photo of yourself as a child. Look at him/her with tenderness.

Speak to that child with the love he/she needs. Tell him/her how beautiful he/she is. Tell him/her you're proud of him/her. Make him/her a promise:

"I will take care of you. No one will hurt you again."

Do this for several days. Little by little, you'll feel that wounded child becoming loved and protected.

Exercise 2: Acknowledge your achievements.

Make a list of all your accomplishments. Remember—you were a champion from the very beginning: you won a race of millions when you reached your mother's egg.

Write it all down: your first steps, your learnings, your brave moments, and the times you kept going despite fear. Recognize yourself.

'You are a miracle in motion.'

Exercise 3: Mirror work

Stand in front of a mirror and look into your eyes. Say out loud: "I'm so proud of you." "I love and accept you just as you are."

"You are enough. You are worthy. You are a perfect creation of God."

Do this daily. Don't wait to *feel* good to do it—do it until you *do* feel good.

Exercise 4: Reprogram your language

Repeat powerful affirmations like:
- "I am enough."
- "My dreams matter."
- "I am worthy, and I deserve the best."
- "Abundance is on its way to me."

A lie repeated many times becomes the truth. So, start repeating new truths that build you up.

Exercise 5: Do what you fear.

Step out of your comfort zone. Do what you used to avoid because of fear or shame. Every time you do, you'll be amazed by your strength. Your self-esteem will grow—because *you'll prove to yourself that you can.* That's real confidence: *the kind you build step by step.*

Exercise 6: Take care of your body and mind.

Move your body, sleep well, eat with love, meditate, and breathe. Surround yourself with people who make you feel good. Celebrate every step, even the smallest. Because **you are worth it**. At the end of each day, hug yourself with your soul and say silently

"Thank you for not giving up. Thank you for continuing.
I'm here for you."
"You didn't come to this world to hide your light.
You came to shine, to be yourself, to walk with
dignity. You are enough. You already are. You just need to
remember it."

Audio to Strengthen Self-Esteem
"Recognize yourself, love yourself, bloom."

This is a recording for you to listen to every day—as often as you can, especially at night before sleep.

Prepare Your Space

Choose a quiet room (no background noise—windows closed, appliances off). Use cushions, curtains, or blankets to absorb sound. Turn off your phone and let others know not to disturb you.

Prepare Your Voice and Energy

Drink water 10–15 minutes before recording. Take deep breaths and smile—your smile is heard in your voice. Read the script silently first to feel the rhythm and flow.

When Recording

Begin with 2 seconds of silence (help in editing later). Speak slowly, with intention. Pause generously where indicated. If you make a mistake, pause, breathe, repeat the sentence, and continue. Don't aim for perfection. What matters most is that it feels real, loving, and yours.

Suggested length: 12–20 minutes

Tone: Warm, empathetic, loving voice

Ideal Music Suggestions for Your Self-Esteem Audio

- Use tracks without sudden volume changes.
- Make sure your voice is always louder than the music.

Leave brief moments of near silence during key affirmations.

1. Emotional and gentle piano

- Conveys intimacy, sensitivity, and self-acceptance.
- Ludovico Einaudi – *"Una Mattina"* or *"Ascolta"*
- (Evocative, emotional—perfect for affirmations and visualizations)
- Kevin Kern – *"Through the Arbor"*

(Ideal for reflective parts—pure and serene)

- Peder B. Helland – *"Calm Piano Music 24/7"*
- (Soft continuous piano background, no surprises)

2. Ambient music with nature sounds

- Perfect for induction and final affirmations.
- Christopher Lloyd Clarke – *"Soothing Sanctuary"* or *"Ascension"*

(Ideal for deep hypnosis and inner healing)

- Liquid Mind – *"Balance"* or *"Reflection"*

(Loving, slow-moving background—no beats)

- Enya instrumental – *"Watermark (Instrumental)"*

(Inner beauty and peace, melodic yet gentle)

3. Special frequencies (optional)

- Used very subtly in the background:
- 528 Hz – Frequency of self-love and emotional healing
- 432 Hz – Emotional harmony and inner peace
Available on: Insight Timer
- Spotify: *"Inner Confidence," "Gentle Piano for Self-Love"*
- YouTube: *"Self-Love Meditation Music – 528Hz + Gentle Piano"*

Induction and Deep Relaxation

Take a deep breath... Inhale through your nose...

And exhale slowly and gently through your mouth...

This moment is just for you...

A space of care, of rest, of reconnection...

Feel relaxed with each breath... Your mind softens...

And your heart gently opens to a new experience of self-love... Now imagine a soft light descending from above...

That light touches the top of your head...

And relaxes your forehead... your eyes... your jaw... your neck... your shoulders...

Your chest and your back...

With every part of your body that relaxes... you feel safer... more held... more at peace...

Transformation—Self-Acceptance and Self-Love

Now imagine you're standing in front of a mirror... But this isn't just any mirror—it's a mirror of the soul.

And in it, you can see not just your outer image...

But everything you are: your story, your values, your dreams, your wounds, your light...

Observe yourself... with tenderness.

No judgment.

Just love.

Maybe for a long time, you spoke to yourself harshly...

You compared yourself...

You demanded perfection...

But today, that ends.

Today, you choose to speak with love.

To treat yourself with respect.

To look at yourself the way you'd look at someone you love deeply.

Repeat silently in your mind:

"I am enough, just as I am."

"I respect myself. I value myself. I see myself."

"I don't need to be perfect to be worthy of love."

Feel these words rooting inside you...

Like seeds of a new inner life...

Where confidence, peace, and trust begin to bloom

Release of Limiting Beliefs

Now imagine you're carrying a suitcase.

Inside are all the words that once hurt you...

Criticism, labels, other people's expectations...

Everything that ever made you doubt yourself...

Feel, just for a moment, how heavy that suitcase is.

And now... decide to let it go. Set it down.

You don't need it anymore. It does not define you.

You are not your mistakes. You are not your fears.

You are a story in transformation...

A light expanding... A worthy, capable, radiant being.

Affirmations and Positive Closing

Repeat silently—pause after each one to feel it fully:

"I accept myself with love, here and now."

"My worth is not defined by others, but by what I recognize in myself."

"Each day, I treat myself with more kindness, more patience, more respect."

"I am blooming. I am growing. I am returning to myself."

Feel these words like inner caresses...

A reconnection to your true self...

Now... slowly...

Bring your attention back to the present...

Wiggle your fingers... your shoulders...

Stretch if you wish...

And when you're ready...

Gently open your eyes...

And return with a new sense of calm, strength, and love for yourself.

CHAPTER 5

ASSUME RESPONSIBILITY

Take Personal Responsibility

Taking personal responsibility is one of the most powerful decisions you can make. It frees you from a victim's mindset and gives you your power back. You stop thinking the world is against you and start asking:

What can *I* do to change this?

Learn from Every Fall

We all make mistakes. No one is perfect. But failure is not the end—it's an opportunity to grow, learn, and evolve. When facing a difficult situation, don't ask:

"Why me?" Instead ask:

"What is this here to teach me? What can I learn?"

Situations are temporary, but the lessons they leave can last a lifetime.

Shift Your Focus

Many people spend years punishing themselves for one mistake. But self-doubt kills more dreams than failure ever will.

If your plan doesn't work, change the plan—not the goal.

Remember: Goals without action are just wishes. Consistency is more powerful than perfection.

Take risks. Let go of guilt, fear, the past, and problems that aren't yours. And above all, stop complaining. Complaining only drains your energy and attracts more negativity.

Communication

Never assume anything. We all listen through the filter of our beliefs and interpretations. Ask. Confirm. Reconfirm.

Poor communication creates misunderstandings. Learn to express yourself—and to truly listen.

Peace comes when you stop letting others control your emotions. You are stronger, braver, and wiser than you think.

Protect Your Environment

Some people radiate light. Others are covered in mud. Those filled with light brighten your home and your path. Those covered in mud stain everything they touch.

They drain your energy, splash you with negativity, and leave the air heavy. Surround yourself only with people who uplift you. Be grateful—and let go of those whose time in your life has ended.

Live Today with Awareness

Spend time with your family. Listen to them. Hug them. It costs nothing… but creates eternal memories. Each day is a gift that will never come again.

Don't Die While You're Still Alive

It's not the body that decays at death—it's the soul when we stop truly living.

Create the Life You Desire

Success isn't about luxury. It's about living without stress, caring for your health, being with the people you love, and enjoying what you do. Do what makes you happy.

If you don't like where you are, move—you're **not a tree.** And don't take life too seriously… Because either way, no one gets out alive.

Let Go of What No Longer Serves You

God puts people in your life—and removes them once you've learned what you needed. You can't start a new chapter if you don't close the last one.

Don't move mountains for someone who wouldn't lift a stone for you.

Learn to say **NO** without guilt.

And walk away from people who only complain, blame, or drain you.

Choose Consciously

Be intentional about who you share your time with. To truly know someone, don't look at their status or clothes—

Watch how they treat others.

The one who talks badly about others…

will eventually talk badly about you too.

" You're not responsible for what happened to you—but you *are* responsible for what you do with it.

And starting today,

You choose to become the architect of your life."

CHAPTER 6

GRATITUDE

Gratitude Changes Everything

Multiple studies have shown that practicing gratitude literally transforms the brain. It increases levels of serotonin and dopamine, the neurotransmitters of well-being—reduces stress and strengthens our ability to make decisions and regulate emotions.

Grateful people tend to be kinder and more compassionate, both with themselves and with others, cultivating deeper and more meaningful relationships.

Gratitude shifts our perspective. It sets us free.

No one owes us anything. Your parents—or whoever raised you—weren't obligated to do it; they did the best they could with the resources they had. Be grateful.

Children don't owe us anything either, so if they call, if they're present, give thanks.

If someone helped you without being obligated to, thank them too. The only true obligation is the one we have to ourselves:

To be aware of how fortunate we truly are.

Everything you have is on loan: your body, your partner, your children, and your belongings. When the time comes to return them, do it with love and gratitude for the time you shared.

Happiness doesn't come from having everything; it comes from being grateful for everything.

A Life Lesson

My sister taught me a powerful lesson about gratitude.

Her son—a young pilot—died in a plane crash. They had a very close relationship. At his funeral, she placed a rose on his casket, raised her arms to the sky, and said,

**"Father, I thank you for the 26 years you lent me my son. I enjoyed him deeply, and I learned from him.
Now I return him to you."**

It left me speechless. Most people drown in grief, but she found peace through gratitude.

Gratitude Helps You Let Go

When a romantic relationship ends, give thanks for what you lived and what you learned. When you lose a material thing, let it go with gratitude for the time it served you.

Attachment chains us and causes suffering.

Your value doesn't lie in what you possess, but in what you are able to release. Happiness is a choice. Somewhere, someone would do anything to have what you have today. Gratitude for what you already have builds resilience, improves relationships, and connects you to abundance.

Feeling rich or poor is an emotional state.

You can have little and feel full or have much and feel empty. The difference lies in where you place your attention.

Gratitude Exercises

- Express gratitude daily—for big and small things.
- Take mindful pauses to reflect on your blessings.
- Before sleep, list at least five things you're grateful for from the day.
- Keep a gratitude journal to record lessons and meaningful moments.

- Write yourself a thank-you letter.
- Practice acts of kindness—donate your time or resources.
- Surround yourself with positive thoughts and eliminate negativity.
- Walk in gratitude, appreciating simple things: the sun, the wind, life itself.
- Acknowledge your accomplishments—value yourself.
- Thank the people around you for their presence, gestures, and love.
- Strengthen your relationships by expressing sincere appreciation.

"The more you give thanks, the more reasons you'll have to be thankful.
Gratitude doesn't change what you have—it changes what you see."

CHAPTER 7

EMPATHY AND COMPASSION

A Lesson in Empathy

A little mouse peeked through a hole in the wall and saw the farmer and his wife setting a mousetrap. Alarmed, he ran into the farmyard to warn all the other animals of the danger.

The chicken replied, "I understand that's a big problem for *you*, but it doesn't affect *me*."

The mouse then went to the lamb, who said, "I'm sorry for you. I'll pray for you."

Desperate, the mouse approached the cow. "And how exactly does that affect *me*?" she replied.

Feeling helpless, the mouse returned to the house, knowing he would have to face the danger alone.

That night, there was a loud sound. The trap had caught something. The farmer's wife rushed to see what it was. In the darkness, she didn't realize the trap had caught the tail of a venomous snake. The snake bit her.

The farmer took her to the hospital, but when they returned, her fever worsened. He killed the chicken to make her soup.

When she didn't improve and family members came to visit, they slaughtered the lamb to feed them. Finally, the woman passed away, and the farmer sold the cow to pay for the funeral.

From his corner, the mouse watched how what seemed to be *his* problem ended up affecting *everyone*.

A Powerful Lesson

This story offers a powerful truth: empathy matters. Many people believe that someone else's problem has nothing to do with them. They ignore others' pain, not realizing that we're all connected. Suffering doesn't stay isolated. What affects one… may eventually affect us all.

What Is Empathy?

Empathy is the ability to put yourself in another's shoes to understand their pain, their perspective, and their story.

Emotional empathy makes us *feel* another's pain as our own. Compassionate empathy moves us to *act*—to relieve that suffering. It is through empathy that compassion is born.

Compassion Is Not Pity

Pity creates distance. It makes us feel superior. Compassion, on the other hand, is rooted in respect and a genuine desire to help from the heart. Empathic people don't just listen. They practice active listening, observe body language, Respect differences, and believe in the essential goodness of others. They don't impose their views—they seek to understand before judging.

Empathy and Compassion Begin with You

We cannot give what we don't have. To truly practice compassion with others, we must first be compassionate with ourselves. Be kind to yourself. Forgive yourself. Hug yourself.

Acknowledge your efforts. Treat yourself the way you'd treat someone you love in a hard moment.

Exercises to Cultivate Empathy and Compassion

Active Listening:

Really pay attention. Don't interrupt. Notice gestures, emotions, and tone.

Perspective Shift:

Put yourself in someone else's shoes. Imagine their story.

Loving-Kindness Meditation:

Repeat: *"May you be well. May you be happy. May you be at peace. May you be free from suffering."*

Self-Compassion:

Treat your mistakes with understanding, like you would with someone you love. Start with yourself, then extend to others.

Find Common Ground:

We all want to love, to feel safe, and to be happy. Focus on what connects you—not what separates you.

Practice Gratitude:

Be grateful for what you have. Be grateful to those around you.

Help Someone or Volunteer: Offering genuine support deepens our connection with others.

Observe and Reflect: Be aware of others' pain. Look with compassionate eyes.

Avoid Judgments:

Challenge your limiting beliefs. Open your heart and mind to others' realities.

Learn About Other Cultures: Read, talk, travel… It all expands your perspective.

Practice Mindfulness:

Being present helps you respond with empathy instead of reacting impulsively.
Be Patient with Yourself:
We're all learning. Be your own safe space.

"You don't need to have the same pain to offer compassion." "You just need to care."
"When the pain of others is not indifferent to you, your soul flourishes in humanity."

CHAPTER 8

FEAR

Understanding Fear

Fear is a natural survival response that helps us face danger. Thanks to it, humans—and animals—have survived millennia.

When a living being perceives a threat, the brain reacts immediately: the amygdala sends an alert signal to the hypothalamus, which activates the nervous and endocrine systems.

As a result, hormones and neurotransmitters are released:

- **Adrenaline**, which heightens alertness
- **Cortisol**, the stress hormone
- **Endorphins**, which calm the body once the threat has passed

Fear shows up as an intense, unpleasant sensation. When it takes over, it's hard to think about anything else. Negative images appear, muscles tense, facial expressions change, hands sweat, the body trembles… Sometimes, we even freeze completely.

Types of Fear

There are two main types of fear:

1. **Irrational fears (or phobias):**

    Fears that don't represent real danger, such as fear of spiders, flying, driving, closed spaces, heights, blood, or thunderstorms.

2. **Rational fears:**

    Based on situations that truly involve a threat, such as falling from a high place, being separated from family, losing control, or facing certain social situations.

The problem begins when fear stops protecting us and starts **limiting us**. It stops being an ally and becomes a powerful enemy.

It sabotages us—disguised as excuses, procrastination, or insecurity—and keeps us from acting.

How many times have you made decisions based on the fear of what others might think?

How many times have you shaped your life around what you believe others expect from you out of fear of being judged?

How to Face Fear

Fear can be transformed. Here's an 8-step path to help you do it:

1. Identify it

Name it. Observe it. Put it into words. Is it real or imaginary?

If you can define the threat and take action to resolve it, it's likely a real fear. If it's vague, anticipatory, or exaggerated, it's probably imaginary.

2. Notice when it appears.

Reflect on the situations that activate it. What triggers it? What keeps it going?

3. Accept your fears.

Don't judge yourself for feeling them. Fear is a human emotion. Accepting it is the first act of courage.

4. Explore its origin.

When did you first feel it? Is it a learned fear?

Sometimes we grow up absorbing others' reactions. For example, if a mother screams at the sight of a spider, her child may associate that with real danger and develop a phobia.

5. Face it gradually.

You don't have to jump into the abyss. You can approach it step by step. Controlled exposure makes you stronger.

6. Breathe

A powerful technique: **box breathing** (four-count breathing): Inhale slowly to a count of four…
Hold for four…
Exhale gently to a count of four… Pause. Then repeat.
This technique activates endorphins and calms the nervous system.

7. Challenge limiting beliefs

What thoughts are feeding that fear? Question them. Ask yourself, "Is **this absolutely true?"**

8. Acknowledge your progress.

Every step forward deserves recognition. Celebrate yourself. You are braver than you think.

"Brave is not he who does not feel fear, but he who faces it."

Where fear ends… magic begins.

CHAPTER 9

PROCRASTINATION

Procrastination: The Art of Delaying Your Life

Procrastination is closely linked to stress, anxiety, sleep problems, and a wide range of mental and physical health challenges caused by the buildup of unfinished tasks.

It's a form of **self-sabotage**; we postpone or avoid important activities, often without a real reason.

There are no magic pills to fix it. Part of the problem is that we become addicted to **instant gratification**, seeking small bursts of dopamine by doing easier or more enjoyable tasks instead.

But meaningful projects require **time, consistency, and patience**. Motivation may appear… but it's temporary. That's why, instead of depending on motivation, we need to develop the habit of **discipline**.

Why Do We Procrastinate?

Identifying the cause is essential. Some common reasons include:

- Fear of failure
- Doubts about our own abilities
- Lack of commitment or motivation
- Anxiety or exhaustion
- Paralyzing perfectionism
- Disorganization
- Emotional dependence on mood ("I'll start when I feel better")

Sometimes we delay important things because we've overcommitted to others. Learning to say "no" **assertively** is key to protecting your time and goals.

And of course, **constant distractions**—like social media—easily divert our attention, making us swap meaningful tasks for quicker, more entertaining ones.

How to Stop Procrastinating

Changing this habit isn't easy—but it is possible. Here's a practical, step-by-step approach:

1. Have a Clear Vision of Your Goal

There are no elevators to success. You climb one step at a time, one day at a time. Wishing is not enough; you must act.

2. Write Down Your Goals

Writing creates a commitment to yourself.
- Make a clear, prioritized list.

- Break down each goal into small, specific tasks.
- Schedule when you'll do each action.

Small daily progress leads to big results.

3. Set a Deadline for Each Task

A defined deadline creates urgency and focus.

4. Create Immediate Rewards

Draw a heart, add a sticker, or praise yourself every time you complete a task. This reinforces your progress and keeps you motivated.

5. Focus on One Thing at a Time

Avoid multitasking. Doing too many things at once scatters your energy. Choose one task, finish it, then move to the next.

6. Use the Pomodoro Technique

- Work with focus for 25 minutes
- Rest for 5 to 10 minutes
- Repeat the cycle

Turn off your phone and set a timer. It's simple—and effective.

7. If It Takes Less Than 2 Minutes… Do It Now

Calls, emails, and small tasks: if you can finish them right away, do it. You'll free up mental space.

8. Have Backup Plans

Prepare for setbacks: What will you do if something

unexpected comes up?

Final Reflection

Many people have a million plans… but they all begin "tomorrow."

And tomorrow doesn't exist.

Procrastination drains your energy, creates guilt, lowers your self-esteem, and delays your dreams.

That's why you must stay organized, act with intention, and be ready when the opportunity arrives. *And most importantly:*

"Don't wait to reach the goal to be happy.
Enjoy the journey on your way there."

CHAPTER 10

INTERNAL DIALOGUE

What Do You Tell Yourself When No One Is Listening?

That voice that echoes in your mind, sometimes soft, sometimes harsh, is with you from the moment you wake up until you fall asleep.
It's your **inner dialogue**.

And though it may seem invisible, it holds incredible power: it shapes your self-esteem, your emotions, your decisions... even the way you live.

What you tell yourself can be your **refuge or your prison**.

Often, we're unaware of how we speak to ourselves. We talk with pressure, disqualify ourselves, and repeat phrases that aren't even ours—inherited from significant adults, cultural messages, or painful experiences.

Phrases like

- "I'm not enough."
- "I always mess everything up."
- "I have no willpower."
- "They're probably judging me."
- "I can't do this."

With repetition, these thoughts become **beliefs**. And beliefs create reality.

Where Does That Voice Come From?

Your inner dialogue is built from childhood. The words you heard, the judgments you received, the comparisons, the expectations placed on you... all of it leaves a mark. And often, that inner voice isn't even yours—it's an **echo of someone else's voice** from when you were vulnerable.

If you grew up surrounded by criticism, you might be overly hard on yourself now. If you were taught to push yourself too much to feel worthy, your inner voice might never let you rest. And if no one ever showed you how to speak to yourself with love, it might feel strange to do it today.

What Happens When We Don't Question That Voice?

We live on autopilot. We accept everything we tell ourselves as **truth**, without realizing that this "narration" might be distorted by fear, insecurity, or unresolved pain. This can lead to:

- Feeling incapable, even when you have the tools
- Delaying your dreams out of fear of failure
- Sabotaging relationships or important decisions
- Increased anxiety, guilt, and stress

What you say to yourself matters more than what others think of you.

Common Examples of Negative Self-Talk

We often repeat phrases on autopilot, unaware of how damaging they are. Some even seem "realistic" but are filled with judgment, fear, or self-rejection.

Examples:
- "I can't do anything right."
- "I'm a mess."
- "This always happens to me."
- "It'll probably go wrong."
- "Why bother? I'll just fail."
- "I'll never change."
- "I have no willpower."
- "I'm just unlucky."

These thoughts, when repeated often, become **limiting beliefs.**

that weaken your confidence and your approach to life.

How to Identify Your Inner Dialogue

The first step is to become aware of it. Start by observing your thoughts in everyday situations—especially when:

- You make a mistake.
- You're about to try something new.

- You receive criticism.
- You feel fear or pressure

Ask yourself:

What am I telling myself right now?

Is this voice helping or sabotaging me? Would I speak like this to someone I love?

A helpful tool is to **write your self-talk in a journal**. Seeing it written out helps you recognize patterns with more clarity.

How to Transform Your Inner Dialogue

This isn't about lying to yourself with fake positivity. It's about speaking your truth—with **compassion**. It's about letting go of inherited or destructive phrases and choosing thoughts that **lift you up** instead of holding you back.

Here are some practical tools:

1. Rewrite Your Thoughts

Take a negative thought and reframe it with a more compassionate, realistic version.

Examples:

- "I never can…" → "I'm learning, and I'm getting closer each time."
- "I'm a failure." → "I made a mistake, but that doesn't define who I am."
- "I'm not good enough." → "I'm learning to recognize my

worth."

2. Create Your Own Affirmations

Choose phrases you want to internalize and repeat them with intention.

Examples:
- "I'm doing the best I can."
- "I allow myself to learn without demanding perfection."
- "I'm capable—even when I'm afraid."
- "I deserve to speak to myself with respect."
- "Each day, I grow closer to my most authentic self."

Say them out loud when you wake up, before bed, or whenever a limiting thought shows up.

3. Keep a Thought Record

For one week, note any recurring negative thoughts. Next to each, write a more loving and balanced version.

This trains your brain to **identify and transform** your internal patterns.

Final Reflection

Your inner voice is always with you. It's the voice you hear when no one else is around. That's why it needs to be a voice that supports you, encourages you, and reminds you of who you are when you forget.

Maybe for years that voice has been harsh, critical, or demanding.

But today, you can choose to change it. It won't happen overnight.

But **every time you choose kindness**, you're healing something inside. You're building a new relationship with yourself.

You are the person you'll spend the most time with in this life. Make sure that relationship is a safe space. You don't need to deny your mistakes or hide your emotions. Just learn to look at yourself with **honesty and respect**.

Because if you're not on your side... Who will be?

"Speaking to yourself with love is not weakness. It is **freedom.**"

CHAPTER 11

The Power of Choice

The Power of Choice

For many years, I believed that life was just happening *to me*. Those circumstances, people, and events held the key to my happiness. I felt at the mercy of others, trapped in automatic reactions, recurring anger, and unresolved guilt. Until one day, a phrase woke me up:

"You can't choose what happens to you, but you can choose how you respond."

That idea opened a door. I realized that every thought, every emotion, and every decision is a choice. And while choosing isn't always easy, it is deeply liberating.

Choosing how to react

When someone hurts you, you can react with rage... or choose to set boundaries with love. When something goes wrong, you can give up... or choose to see the lesson. When you make a mistake, you can punish yourself... or choose forgiveness and growth. We can't always choose what others say or do.

But we *can* choose what we do with it.

The sacred space between stimulus and response

Psychologist Viktor Frankl said a phrase that marked my path:

"Between stimulus and response, there is a space. In that space lies our power to choose."

That space exists. I discovered it when I stopped reacting as if on autopilot and started breathing before responding. When I observed my emotions without letting them take over. When I chose to respond from my awareness, not from my wounds.

<u>**Guided Practice: Breathe, Observe, Choose**</u>

Next time something triggers you, try this:

1. Take a deep breath.
2. Notice what you're feeling—without judgment.
3. Choose how you want to respond.

This simple habit can transform your relationships, your inner dialogue, and your peace.

Not choosing is also a choice.

Staying where you're unhappy, staying silent when you want to speak, repeating harmful patterns... Those are also choices. When I understood this, I stopped blaming my past, my circumstances, or others. I took back the wheel of my life.

Choose from love, not fear.

Every day, whether we notice or not, we choose what to think. What to remember. What to feed our heart and mind.

Today, I choose:
- To be my own ally.
- To respond with compassion.
- To release resentment.
- To build my present with intention.

You can choose, too. Because the power of choice is already within you—here, now.

Guided Practice: I Choose with Awareness

This exercise helps you connect to your inner power, even in the midst of chaos or doubt.

1. Close your eyes and breathe.

Take three deep breaths. Inhale through your nose, exhale through your mouth. Let your body relax and your mind soften.

2. Recall a recent situation.

Think of something that bothered or upset you. It doesn't have to be big. Just observe it.

3. **Ask yourself:**
- How did I react at that moment?
- Was it calm, or from my wounds?
- What emotion was strongest—fear, anger, sadness, or confusion?

Observe without judging.

4. **Now imagine that same moment… but with a new response.**

From the wisdom you have today. From the person you're becoming.
- What new choice would you make?
- How would you respond now?
- What emotion would guide you—peace, empathy, clarity, or love?

Feel that new choice in your body. Make it real in your mind and heart.

5. **Anchor your choice with a phrase.**

Write it down, say it out loud, or repeat it in your mind. Here are some ideas:
- "I choose to act from my inner power."
- "I respond with love, not fear."
- "I have the power to choose how I live each moment." Say it three times—and feel it deeply.

6. Give thanks and return slowly.

Thank yourself for this conscious pause.

Come back to the present, knowing that with each new day…

You choose your path.

CHAPTER 12

THE POWER OF THE PRESENT

"The Only Real Moment"

We spend much of our lives trapped in memories of the past or worried about a future that doesn't yet exist. Without realizing it, we miss the only moment we truly have: the now.

I, too, spent years disconnected from the present. I would relive old wounds, project my fears, and obsessively plan, always waiting for life to begin after something happened. But one day, I understood: everything I was seeking—peace, love, fulfillment—could only be found **here and now**.

What does it mean to live in the present?

Living in the present doesn't mean ignoring the past or never planning. It means being conscious, aware, and open to what's happening at this moment, without judgment.

It means truly savoring a cup of coffee. Listening with your whole being. Feeling the sun on your skin. Breathing with intention. It means coming home to yourself again and again with each breath.

The effects of disconnecting from now

When we're not present, we often feel:
- Anxiety about the future
- Guilt and regret about the past
- Emotional disconnection
- Living on autopilot

We lose the sacredness of the moment and become prisoners of a restless mind.

Keys to reconnect with the present

1. **Conscious breathing**

Close your eyes. Breathe. Feel the air coming in and out. That's presence, always available, always real.

2. **Non-judgmental observation**

Notice what's happening inside and around you, without needing to change it. Acceptance is freedom.

3. **Anchoring your body**

Walk barefoot. Feel your heartbeat. Move with intention. Your body is always here, always now.

4. **One thing at a time**

Eat, speak, work... do it with full awareness. Every action becomes an invitation to return to yourself.

5. **Pause throughout the day.**

Create mini rituals: stop, breathe, feel, and give thanks.

Come back to now.

Practical Exercise: The Sacred Minute

Take 60 seconds. Just breathe. Observe. Do nothing else. Just be.

Try this several times a day. You'll begin to notice your energy, your mind, and your heart shifting.

Personal Reflection

The present moment has saved me from unnecessary pain. It has brought peace where there once was anxiety. It gave me back the power to steer my life.

Now I know I don't need to have everything figured out to feel okay. I just need to be **here now.**

Anchor phrases to stay present.

- "The present moment is a gift. That's why it's called the present."
- "Only here can I create, heal, and love."
- "My peace is not in tomorrow or yesterday—it's in this exact moment."

Closing: The Now as a Path of Transformation

Everything begins now: your healing, your freedom, and your power. You don't need to rush, fix everything, or know exactly what to do. You only need to be here. Because at this moment—and only in this one—you can choose a new path.

Everything begins now—your healing, your freedom, your power.

CHAPTER 13

IMPORTANCE OF HEALTHY BOUNDARIES

The Importance of Healthy Boundaries

For many years, I believed that being a good person meant saying yes to everything. I often placed others' needs above my own, afraid that if I dared to say no, I'd be rejected, criticized, or judged. I lived constantly crossing my own limits—and slowly, it drained my energy and silenced my voice.

One day, I realized that setting boundaries wasn't selfish; it was responsible. That taking care of myself didn't make me less generous but more whole. That true love for others and for myself could not exist without respect.

This chapter is an invitation to give yourself permission. Permission to protect yourself, to choose yourself, to say no without guilt, and to understand that you don't need to justify prioritizing your well-being. Because when you are well, everything in your life begins to bloom with greater harmony.

Setting healthy boundaries is an act of love.

Love for your time.

Love for your peace.

Love for your life.

1. The Art of Protecting Yourself with Love

Healthy boundaries are essential for emotional, physical, and spiritual well-being. "Saying no to others is sometimes saying yes to yourself." Setting boundaries isn't selfish; it's an act of self-love and responsibility.

2. What Are Healthy Boundaries?

Healthy boundaries are emotional, physical, mental, and spiritual barriers that protect your integrity without harming others.

They:

- Prevent emotional burnout.
- Strengthen self-esteem.
- Encourage balanced relationships.

Examples: not answering messages outside your schedule, asking for respectful communication, and reserving personal time.

3. Why Is It So Hard to Set Boundaries?

Some common reasons:

- Fear of rejection or conflict.

- Guilt.
- Childhood conditioning (pleasing, avoiding conflict).
- Manipulative or abusive relationships.
- Low self-esteem.
- Belief that your needs matter less than others'.
- Belief that saying no is selfish.

It was hard for me too, until I began loving and accepting myself and realized that I alone was responsible for my life.

4. The Transformational Power of Boundaries

When you set boundaries:
- You reclaim your energy.
- You feel safer and more empowered.
- You stop absorbing others' emotions.
- You become more authentic.

Imagine your mind as "a house with doors and windows—you get to decide what comes in and what stays out."

5. How to Know When You Need Boundaries

- You feel constant discomfort, exhaustion, or frustration.
- Certain people give you anxiety.
- You have no time for yourself.
- You feel used or undervalued.

6. Practical Exercises for Setting Boundaries

Exercise 1: Choose one situation where you need a boundary. Describe what's happening, how you feel, and how you'd like to respond. Then write a clear and loving sentence to express that boundary.

Exercise 2: Protective Sphere Visualization

Imagine a bright light surrounding and protecting you from everything that doesn't belong to you. You can do this at the start of your day or before difficult meetings.

Exercise 3: Yes & No List

Create two columns:
- What you say YES to (your time, respect, rest).
- What you say NO to (guilt, abuse, overcommitment).

7. Inspirational Phrases to Support Your Boundaries

Affirmations to repeat:
- "I have the right to protect my energy."
- "Setting boundaries doesn't make me a bad person—it sets me free."
- "I can be loving without being a people-pleaser."

8. Choosing Yourself Is an Act of Love

Setting boundaries doesn't push the right people away; it invites healthier relationships. Commit to your well-being and practice self-care without guilt. "Boundaries are bridges to freedom, not walls of isolation."

Conclusion: Choosing Yourself Is Love

Setting healthy boundaries isn't a rejection of others; it's a deep yes to your peace, your well-being, and your authenticity.

It's not about building walls but about drawing clear paths that show where your giving ends—without losing yourself in the process.

It's about honoring your time, your emotions, and your energy.

When you choose yourself, something shifts: you begin attracting healthier connections. You feel lighter. And you live with more clarity.

Saying no to others is sometimes saying yes to yourself.
And that, dear reader, is a profound act of self-love.

CHAPTER 14

INSOMNIA

When Rest Slips Away

Few things are as frustrating as wanting to sleep… and not being able to. The mind doesn't stop. The body is exhausted, yet thoughts keep running as if it were the middle of the day. You toss and turn in bed, check the clock, count sheep, take deep breaths… and nothing works. The night goes on, and you remain awake, trapped in a cycle that seems endless.

Insomnia doesn't just steal your sleep. It also takes away your calm, your energy, your focus, and your good mood. When sleepless nights accumulate, life itself begins to lose its brightness. Emotions become more intense, anxiety sets in, and the body starts to suffer.

In my practice, I've seen many people come in with that same tired look in their eyes, searching for a solution. Some have gone weeks without sleeping well; others, years. Many have tried everything: pills, herbal teas, techniques, apps… And while some things help temporarily, the insomnia returns. That's because the problem isn't only in the body: it's in the mind, in the soul, in what hasn't yet been healed.

Throughout this chapter, I want to share a deeper perspective on insomnia. Not as an enemy, but as a message. A signal from the body telling us that something inside needs to be heard, understood, and released. From my experience with clinical hypnosis, I've learned that true rest begins when we feel safe, at peace, and balanced within.

Sleeping shouldn't be a struggle. Sleep is an act of self-love, of trusting surrender. And you, too, can return to sleeping peacefully.

Why Does Insomnia Appear?

Insomnia isn't just difficulty falling asleep. It can also be waking up in the middle of the night with a racing mind, or opening your eyes too early, heart pounding, feeling like you haven't rested at all.

There are different types of insomnia:
- Onset insomnia: when it's hard to fall asleep.
- Maintenance insomnia: when you wake up several times during the night.
- Early morning awakening: when you wake up too early and can't go back to sleep.

Each form has its own root, but they all share one truth: something inside you doesn't feel completely safe, calm, or at peace.

Often, insomnia reflects an overloaded mind, unprocessed emotions, or worries that remain active even as you try to rest. It can appear after a significant life change, a loss, a period of stress, accumulated anxiety, or even habits that disrupt the body's natural rhythm, like excessive screen time, caffeine, or repetitive thoughts.

But beyond external causes, insomnia often has a deeper origin: a part of you that resists letting go of control, that fears disconnection, that associates rest with vulnerability. That part, often unconscious, needs to feel safe to surrender to sleep.

From my experience as a hypnotherapist, I've seen how insomnia can be a call from the soul. A signal that there are stored emotions, unresolved stories, and inner voices that don't allow the silence needed for sleep. And that's where healing begins, not just by quieting the mind, but by listening to what needs attention.

Sleeping well isn't just a biological matter. It's also emotional, mental, and spiritual balance. And, when we understand it this way, we stop fighting insomnia and start understanding what it's truly trying to tell us.

The Role of the Subconscious Mind and Clinical Hypnosis

Most people try to solve insomnia from the conscious mind: applying techniques, changing routines, and reading advice. And while all of that can be helpful, it's often not enough. Because insomnia doesn't originate on the surface... it originates deep within.

Our conscious mind represents only a small part of who we are. It's the part that reasons, analyzes, and plans. But beneath it lies the subconscious mind, where our deepest beliefs, repressed emotions, memories, and oldest patterns reside. And it's there, in many cases, that insomnia takes root.

The subconscious mind has one mission: to protect us. And if at some point in your life you associated rest with danger, abandonment, anxiety, or the feeling of losing control, that part of you will do everything possible to keep you alert... even when you want to sleep.

In clinical hypnosis sessions, I've guided people who, without realizing it, had been carrying unconscious fears, past traumas, or inner voices repeating, "You can't relax," "It's not safe to let your guard down," or "If you fall asleep, something bad might happen." And when these beliefs are brought to light and transformed with love, the body can finally rest.

Clinical hypnosis isn't magic; it's a powerful tool of self-connection. It allows gentle access to the root of the problem, reprograms the subconscious mind, and plants new associations: rest as safety, sleep as well-being, and nighttime as a space of peace.

During a session, I guide the person into a deep state of relaxation, where their mind is more receptive. In that state, we work with images, emotions, and positive suggestions that re-educate the relationship with sleep. It's a respectful, natural, and deeply liberating process.

Sleep is not just about closing your eyes. It's about trust. It's about letting go of the day, surrendering to the present, and allowing your body and mind to regenerate. And when the subconscious mind learns that it's safe to do so, insomnia loses its power.

The Power of Nighttime Rituals

Sleep doesn't come by force. It arrives by invitation. And that invitation is built.

In a fast-paced world, many people come to bed with a cluttered mind, a tense body, and a restless soul. They expect sleep to come like a switch that turns off instantly. But sleep is a process, not an event. And like any process, it requires preparation, gentleness, and consistency.

Throughout my journey as a therapist, I've seen how a few simple changes can make a big difference in sleep quality. Here are some nighttime rituals you can adopt in your life:

1. **Create a sacred sleep space**: Make your bedroom a calm refuge. Dim the lights, ventilate the room, and tidy up the space. Let your bed be not just a place to sleep, but a sanctuary for reconnecting with yourself.

2. **Disconnect from screens at least an hour before bed**: The blue light from devices disrupts melatonin production, the body's natural sleep hormone. Turning off your phone, TV, or computer before bed is a profound act of self-care.

3. **Practice conscious breathing**: Conscious breathing calms the nervous system. You can try the 4-7-8 technique (inhale for 4 seconds, hold for 7, exhale for 8) or simply focus on your inhalation and exhalation for a few minutes, allowing your body to relax with each cycle.

4. **Liberating journaling**: Before going to bed, write down everything that's on your mind: worries, to-do lists, emotions. It's a way of emptying the mind and letting go of what you no longer need to carry into the night.

5. **Guided visualization**: Imagine a safe, peaceful place: a forest, a beach, or a secret garden. Picture yourself there, in peace, breathing slowly. This exercise activates positive

emotions and signals to your subconscious that it's safe to relax.

6. **Nighttime gratitude**: Take a moment to acknowledge something good from your day. It could be a smile, a gesture, or a small achievement. This simple habit shifts the emotional tone with which you enter rest.

7. **A healing phrase before sleep**: Silently repeat an affirmation like, "I am safe. I deserve to rest. I surrender to sleep with trust and gratitude."

These rituals, though simple, have a profound impact. They teach the body and mind to associate nighttime with calm, and little by little, they reprogram your relationship with rest. Sleeping isn't about giving in to exhaustion; it's about coming home to yourself.

Create Your Own Audio for Deep Sleep

Sleep shouldn't be a battle. Yet, for many people, nighttime becomes a stage for repetitive thoughts, accumulated tensions, and unprocessed emotions.

As a hypnotherapist, I've helped many people reconnect with rest, and today I want to share with you a simple, effective, and deeply loving tool: your own sleep audio.

Recording your voice can be a powerful act of self-compassion. It's like giving yourself a hug at the end of the day.

A Small Ritual Before Bed

Before listening to your audio, create a restful environment. This small ritual will help signal to your body that it's time to let go:

1. Turn off bright lights and light a dim lamp or a candle.
2. Disconnect from screens at least an hour before bed.
3. If you'd like, write down three things you're grateful for today.
4. Do a few gentle stretches or take a deep breath.
5. Settle into bed with the intention of rest, not struggle.

How to Record Your Audio

- Use your phone with a voice recording app.
- Speak slowly, as if you were talking to someone you love.
- Leave long pauses between phrases.
- If you wish, you can add soft background music or nature sounds.

Ideal Music Types

1. **Nature sounds**
- Gentle ocean waves
- Light rain
- Night forest (crickets, leaves rustling)

- A soft river or stream
- Wind in the meadow

Perfect for creating a sense of refuge and connection to the earth.

2. **Frequencies for sleep**

- 432 Hz: Deep relaxation and inner connection.
- 528 Hz: Love, healing, and regeneration.
- Delta Waves (0.5 – 4 Hz): Associated with deep, restorative sleep. **Where to Find Them**

You can search on:

- YouTube: Type "432 Hz sleep music," "delta waves for sleep," or "nature sounds 8 hours."
- Spotify / Apple Music: Look for playlists like "Deep Sleep," "Healing Frequencies," or "Calm Piano for Sleep."
- Apps like Insight Timer, Calm, or Relax Melodies also let you mix sounds or choose long tracks for sleep.

Suggested Script: "Your Night of Deep Rest"

(Feel free to use it as is or adapt it with your own words.)

Introduction—A Loving Welcome Message

- "Hello, it's me...

I'm here to help myself rest.

This is my night… my moment to let go…

There's nothing to solve now…

Just being here… with myself… in calm.

Breathing—The Gateway to Rest

- "I gently close my eyes...

I inhale through my nose...

And exhale slowly through my mouth...

With each exhalation, I let go of the day...

I inhale calm... I exhale tension...

Everything is okay."

Body Relaxation

- "I bring my attention to my feet... to my legs... to my back... arms and shoulders... my neck..." Relax my whole body...

Guided Visualization

- "I imagine myself floating on a soft cloud...

It holds me with love...

The sky is deep and serene...

Nothing worries me...

I let myself be carried away...

Each breath takes me deeper... closer to sleep..."

Positive Reprogramming Phrases

- "My body knows how to rest...

I let go of what I don't need...

Sleep embraces me gently...

I am at peace... I am safe...

Sleep is safe... Sleep is natural...

My body knows how to rest…

I trust in my natural ability to sleep deeply…

I release all worries…

I am safe…

I am at peace…

Sleep comes to me easily…"

Closing – Entering Sleep

"You can let these words fade away…

Your mind doesn't need to do anything else…

Your subconscious will continue listening…

While you simply… drift into sleep…"

You can record yourself reading this script with your gentle voice, or read it silently each night, allowing your subconscious to receive the message.

Remember: sleeping is not about disconnecting. It's about reconnecting with yourself. And each night is a new opportunity to do so with tenderness and trust.

Sleeping in peace is your right, and
You are reclaiming it.

CHAPTER 15

GOODBYE TO CIGARETTES, HELLO TO YOU

"I've walked alongside many people on the path of saying goodbye to cigarettes, and in every story, I discovered it's not just about a habit... It's about an emotional relationship that, once released, makes space to reconnect with oneself."

The Cigarette as a False Refuge

A brief yet clear explanation of how cigarette addiction works not only on a physical level but also emotionally. Mention the most common beliefs:

"It calms me."

"It gives me a moment for myself." "I can't function without it."

What You're Really Looking For

Explore the idea that cigarettes often represent an unmet need:

- Peace
- Pause
- Connection
- Control

And how those needs can begin to be met from within, with self-love and awareness.

Visualize Yourself Free

Here you can include short, guided exercise (like light hypnosis or meditation), where you imagine yourself as someone free from smoking—breathing fully, feeling proud and clear.

"Close your eyes for a moment.
Imagine 21 days have passed without smoking. You breathe with ease.
You feel strong, in control.
What else has changed in your life?"

What You Gain by Saying Goodbye
Create a positive list and write a short, short list of the benefits of quitting smoking—both physical and emotional:
- Better health and energy
- Self-control
- Personal pride
- Being a role model for others
- Emotional freedom
- Include phrases like
- Saving Money

"You're not losing a cigarette—you're reclaiming your power."

Practical Tools to Quit Smoking

You can include here:
- Breathing techniques
- Conscious habit replacement
- Positive anchors (like a gesture to remind yourself you are free)
- Use of affirmations
- Suggestion for therapeutic or hypnosis-based support

Powerful Affirmations

"I choose to care for myself and breathe freedom." "Every day I am freer."

"I don't need to smoke to shine."

"Saying goodbye to cigarettes is so much more than quitting smoking. It's opening the door to a healthier, clearer, freer version of yourself. You're not alone. You can do this.

Hello to you."

<u>Exercises to Quit Smoking</u>

Quitting smoking isn't just about resisting an urge—it's about transforming a relationship. That's why I'm sharing with you a few exercises that can help you reconnect with yourself, reprogram your mind, and walk firmly toward your freedom.

1. The Farewell Ritual

Write a letter to the cigarette as if it were a relationship you're ending. Be honest. Tell it what it meant to you, what it gave you — but also what it took from you. Thank it, if you need to... and then say goodbye.

You can read this letter out loud and burn it (in a safe place) as a symbolic act of closure.

"I don't need you anymore." I choose me."

2. Breathe Freedom

Each time you feel the urge to smoke, pause for a moment. Close your eyes and do the following breathing technique:

- Inhale deeply for 4 counts, imagining you're breathing in freedom.
- Hold the air for 4 counts, feeling your inner power.
- Exhale for 6 counts, releasing anxiety, dependency, and the craving.

Do these 3 times in a row. You'll feel calm and in control—without needing to smoke.

3. Empowerment Anchor

Choose a simple physical gesture (like touching your thumb and index finger together or placing your hand over your heart). Each time you say a positive affirmation or visualize yourself free, do that gesture. Over time, your brain will associate the movement with a sense of strength and freedom. Use it whenever the temptation to smoke appears.

4. Habit Replacement

Identify the most frequent moments when you tend to smoke (e.g., after coffee, after meals, while driving). Then, create a new action to replace it:

• Instead of smoking after coffee, take a 5-minute walk or listen to a calming song.

• Instead of smoking due to stress, take 10 deep breaths or write down how you feel.

• Instead of smoking out of boredom, play a mental game, make a gratitude list, or stretch your body.

Additional tips:
• Set small rewards for yourself.
• Make a list of reasons why you want to quit smoking.
• Some studies show that even smoking **one** cigarette after quitting increases the risk of relapse by 90%.
• If you feel an intense craving, hold a cigarette in your

hand, look at it, and say:

"I'm no longer your slave. I'm free from you. You won't manipulate me again." Then throw it away. It's not about "removing"; it's about **replacing with awareness**.

5. Daily Visualization: You, Free

Every day, take 5 minutes to close your eyes and visualize yourself as someone completely free from cigarettes. Picture yourself breathing with strength, with joy. Feel your body cleaner, your mind clearer. See yourself happy, vibrant, full of energy. Do it **as if** you've already succeeded. Repeat this phrase:

"I am free. My body and mind thank me."

Understanding the Process

During the first 72 hours, your body eliminates nicotine. This stage is critical and may bring intense withdrawal symptoms: anxiety, irritability, insomnia, increased appetite, and a strong urge to smoke.

- **12 hours after quitting:** Carbon monoxide levels in your blood return to normal.
- **2 weeks to 3 months after quitting:** Circulation improves and lung function increases.
- **1 to 9 months after quitting:** Coughing and

shortness of breath begin to improve.

Nicotine withdrawal usually disappears completely within **2 to 3 weeks**. And then… you'll truly feel **free**.

Inspirational Closing

Quitting smoking is not just about putting out a habit. It's about **igniting your light**.

It's looking at yourself with compassion, recognizing your wounds, your efforts, your falls… and still choosing yourself.

It's saying:

"I no longer need to harm myself to feel calm.

I can take care of myself. I am vibrant, and I can hold myself.

I can breathe freedom."

Sometimes we believe we need something external to feel okay. But when you choose to stop smoking, what you're really doing is coming home to your body, to your presence, to your power to choose each step of your life.

You might feel fear. You might think you can't. But let me tell you something: **You can.** Because you already are.

You made it here. You opened this chapter. You've started to look within.

Each smoke-free breath is a **yes** to your life. Each time you choose not to smoke, you're saying:

"I deserve to feel well."

And that... **changes everything**.

So, if you ever doubt, remember this: You're not losing anything. You're gaining clarity, strength, health, self-esteem... You're reclaiming your air.

Your energy. Your time.

You're coming back to **you**.

Goodbye, cigarette...
Hello, you.

Guided Meditation: I Breathe Freedom

Here are two scripts you can record—one is for guided meditation with your voice, and the other is for self-hypnosis.

Step-by-Step Guide to Record Your Guided Meditation at Home

1. Prepare Your Space
- Choose a quiet space, free from background noise (close windows, turn off appliances).
- Use cushions, curtains, or blankets to absorb sound

and reduce echo.

• Turn off your phone and let others in the house know not to interrupt while recording.

2. Prepare Your Equipment

You don't need a professional studio. Here are your options:

Option A: Recording with Your Phone

• Use headphones with a good-quality built-in mic.

• Recommended apps: *Voice Record Pro* (iOS/Android) or any high-quality recorder (.wav or .m4a, not .amr).

• Set the app to record in high quality (at least 44.1 kHz).

Option B: Recording with a Computer

• Plug in an external USB mic (like Blue Yeti, Fifine, or Samson).

• Use the free software *Audacity* (Windows/Mac/Linux):

    o https://www.audacityteam.org/

    o Set your mic to "Mono" and quality to "44100 Hz, 16 bit.""

3. Prepare Your Voice and Energy

• Drink water 10–15 minutes beforehand.

• Take a few deep breaths and smile (it can be heard, even if it's not seen).

- Read the script softly first to get familiar with rhythm and pauses.

4. Record

- Start with 2 seconds of silence (help with editing later).
- Read slowly and intentionally. Pauses were indicated.
- If you make a mistake, just breathe, repeat the phrase, and continue (you can edit it later).

Don't aim for perfection. Focus on making it feel authentic, loving, and *yours*.

5. Add Background Music *(optional but recommended)*

- Use soft, royalty-free instrumental music. Options:
    - YouTube Audio Library o
    - FreeSound.org o
    - Pixabay Music
- In *Audacity*, import the music file and adjust the volume to be very soft (suggested: around -25 dB).

Suggested duration: 5 to 7 minutes

Record with soft background music, and speak in a warm, calm tone.

Audio Script – I Breathe Freedom

Estimated length: 6–7 minutes

Record it in a soft, calm, warm, and confident voice. voice.

Background: Ambient music (piano, bowls, nature) Best for

early morning, bedtime, or moments of anxiety

[**Start—soft—soft music fades in**]

Hello…

Thank you for giving yourself this moment. Today, you're going to breathe… freedom. [**Pause—3—3 sec**]

Find a comfortable position.

Close your eyes… if you feel safe.

And simply… begin to breathe.

No effort… just awareness. [**Pause – 5 sec**]

Inhale… slow and deep.

Exhale… soft, very soft. [**Pause—3sec**]

With every breath… your body relaxes a little more… and your mind begins to quiet. [**Pause—4sec**]

Now…

Imagine the air you breathe in… is clean, pure, and full of life.

And the air you breathe out…

carries away stress, anxiety… and every need to smoke.

[**Pause – 5 sec**]

Inhale freedom… Exhale the past.

Inhale calm… Exhale attachment. Inhale strength… Exhale the cigarette.

[**Pause—6—6sec**]

- Read the script softly first to get familiar with rhythm and pauses.

4. Record

- Start with 2 seconds of silence (help with editing later).
- Read slowly and intentionally. Pauses were indicated.
- If you make a mistake, just breathe, repeat the phrase, and continue (you can edit it later).

Don't aim for perfection. Focus on making it feel authentic, loving, and *yours*.

5. Add Background Music *(optional but recommended)*

- Use soft, royalty-free instrumental music. Options:
    - YouTube Audio Library o
    - FreeSound.org o
    - Pixabay Music
- In *Audacity*, import the music file and adjust the volume to be very soft (suggested: around -25 dB).

Suggested duration: 5 to 7 minutes

Record with soft background music, and speak in a warm, calm tone.

Audio Script – I Breathe Freedom

Estimated length: 6–7 minutes

Record it in a soft, calm, warm, and confident voice. voice.

Background: Ambient music (piano, bowls, nature) Best for

early morning, bedtime, or moments of anxiety

[**Start—soft—soft music fades in**]

Hello…

Thank you for giving yourself this moment. Today, you're going to breathe… freedom. [**Pause—3—3 sec**]

Find a comfortable position.

Close your eyes… if you feel safe.

And simply… begin to breathe.

No effort… just awareness. [**Pause – 5 sec**]

Inhale… slow and deep.

Exhale… soft, very soft. [**Pause—3sec**]

With every breath… your body relaxes a little more… and your mind begins to quiet. [**Pause—4sec**]

Now…

Imagine the air you breathe in… is clean, pure, and full of life.

And the air you breathe out…

carries away stress, anxiety… and every need to smoke.

[**Pause – 5 sec**]

Inhale freedom… Exhale the past.

Inhale calm… Exhale attachment. Inhale strength… Exhale the cigarette.

[**Pause—6—6sec**]

Feel... how each breath cleanses you. Reconnects you. Empowers you. [**Pause—4sec**]

Now... visualize in front of you... a version of yourself that no longer smokes.

Observe them. Breathe like they do. Walk like they do. Smile like they do. [**Pause—6sec**]

That person... is you.

And they are full of energy, clarity... and freedom. [**Pause—4sec**]

Walk toward them.

Look into their eyes.

And listen...

Listen to what they want to tell you. [**Pause—6sec**]

Maybe they say:

"I did it... because I chose me." [**Pause – 5 sec**]

Feel those words in your chest... like a seed beginning to grow. A new version of you... already awakening. [**Pause – 5 sec**]

Now... repeat with me, silently or out loud:

I choose to care for myself.

I choose to release what harms me.

I am free. I am strong. I am me. [**Pause—6sec**]

Place your hand over your heart... and breathe... one more time.

Slow... deep... present. [**Pause—6sec**]

Every breath...

is a declaration of life.

Every choice... brings you closer to you. [**Pause – 5 sec**]

Thank you for giving yourself this moment.

Keep trusting.

Keep breathing.

You are already walking toward your freedom. [**End—music gently fades out**]

Guided Meditation Script – I Breathe Freedom

Close your eyes... and bring your attention to your breath.

Don't change it... just observe.

Inhale slowly... and exhale gently.

Feel the air flowing in and out of your body.

Now, with each inhale... imagine you're breathing in freedom.

With each exhale... release attachment, anxiety, and the past.

Inhale... freedom.

Exhale... the cigarette.

Inhale... strength.

Exhale... dependence.

Inhale... calm.

Exhale... guilt.

Feel how each breath is cleansing your body. Your mind is becoming clearer. Your heart is becoming lighter.

Now visualize a version of yourself who has already quit smoking.

See them… Take a deep breath.

They are radiant, with a real smile, full of vitality. They feel at peace… free… confident.

Watch how they walk, how they breathe, and how they look in the mirror.

That person… is you.

Move closer to them.

Ask: *What did you do to get there?* Listen to their answer… Maybe it surprises you.

Maybe they just say:

"I chose to love myself."

Now, repeat these affirmations—in your mind or out loud:

"I choose to care for myself. I choose to release what harms me."

"I am free. I am strong. I am me."

"I don't need to smoke to shine."

Feel the power of this decision in your chest. Place your hand over your heart... and take one last deep breath.

When you're ready... Slowly open your eyes... And remember: this moment is yours.

Each breath, each choice, brings you closer to you.

"Thank you for giving yourself this moment.
Trust in yourself. You are already walking toward your freedom."

CHAPTER 16

FREE YOURSELF FROM EXCESS WEIGHT

This chapter is not a diet. It's not a manual for counting calories. It's an invitation to reconnect with yourself, to discover what needs you're truly trying to fulfill through food—and to make a brave decision: **to choose your freedom.**

What Are You Really Feeding?

Sometimes we eat because of anxiety, loneliness, boredom, or sadness. Food becomes instant comfort—but also a prison disguised as pleasure.

Learning to observe your emotions before eating can be eye-opening: **Do I feel real hunger… or an emotional void?**

The Body as a Reflection of the Soul

Your body holds your story. Every extra pound may be an armor, a shield, or a silent cry for help. When you begin to honor your body with love, conscious movement, and real nourishment, healing begins from the inside out. It's not about punishment.

It's about **care.**

The Power of Your Mind

With clinical hypnotherapy, I've seen how people can transform their relationship with food from deep within. When you change limiting beliefs like *"I can't," "I'll never make it,"* and *"this is just who I am,"* you open the path to a new inner dialogue—one that's kinder, more powerful, and fully committed to your well-being.

Practical Exercise: Liberating Visualization

Close your eyes and take a deep breath. Imagine you're carrying a heavy backpack.

Inside it are all the emotions, habits, and thoughts that have contributed to your excess weight. Feel the weight of it…

Now decide to release it.

Visualize yourself light, agile, and free.

Walk toward your most vibrant and loving self.

Reflection Questions

- What emotions are you hiding behind food?
- What part of you is asking for attention?
- What does it mean to you to feel light—in body and soul?

Inspirational Quote

"When you choose to love yourself, the body responds. When you release the past, the weight follows."

Weight Loss Audio: "Choose Your Freedom, Release Emotional Weight"

Here is a clean, ready-to-record script, with clear structure and suggested pauses. You may record it with soft background music (relaxing tones like 432 Hz, nature sounds, or gentle piano), keeping a **warm, slow, and soothing tone**.

Suggested Background Music for Your Recording

Soft and Emotive Piano (minimal, heart-centered) Perfect to create warmth without distracting from the words.

Examples:

- *"Weightless Piano"* by Michael FK
- *"Peaceful Piano"* by Ludovico Einaudi (e.g., "Nuvole Bianche" at very low volume)

Solfeggio Frequencies (528 Hz or 432 Hz)

- **528 Hz** is associated with DNA healing, transformation, and miracles.
- **432 Hz** harmonizes body and mind—ideal for hypnotherapy.

You can find these on platforms like:

- YouTube
- Insight Timer
- iTunes

- Spotify

Examples:
- *"528 Hz – Transformational Healing Music"*
- *"432 Hz – Deep Sleep & Healing Music"*

Nature Sounds + Relaxing Pads

· Perfect if you want a more ethereal and enveloping background.

· Example: "Inner Peace" by Christopher Lloyd Clarke, "Floating," or "Deep in the Forest" by Liquid Mind (soft atmospheres without a marked rhythm)

· Environments without marked melody (ideal to keep attention to your voice)

· Soft "ambient" type music, without rhythm or leading instruments

   o "Calm Light" by Peder B. Helland

   o "Meditative State" by Kevin MacLeod (free license for commercial use)

Mixing Tips:

· Keep the music very low (like a whisper in the background), preventing it from competing with your voice.

· Leave spaces of soft silence for pauses and key moments (for example, when you mention "drop the backpack" or "choose your freedom").

- You can use tools like Audacity, GarageBand, or Adobe Audition to mix music and voice with good quality.

Audio Script – Choose Your Freedom: Release Emotional Weight

Duration: 6–8 minutes

Tone: Soft, nurturing, slow, and grounded

Best listened to in the morning, before sleep, or during moments of emotional hunger

[**Soft music fades in—gentle** piano or 432 Hz background.]

Hello…

Thank you for giving yourself this moment.

Today, we're going to release the emotional weight… and connect with your freedom.

[Pause—3sec]

Find a comfortable position. Allow your body to relax.

Close your eyes… if you feel safe to do so.

Begin to breathe… gently, naturally.

Without forcing. Just being present.

[Pause – 5 sec]

Inhale… slowly.

Exhale… deeply.

Feel the air as it moves through you.

With every breath… allow yourself to come home.

[Pause—4sec]

Now...

Bring your attention to your body. Not to judge it—but to feel it.

This is the body that carries you, that holds your story, that has protected you—even with the extra weight.

[Pause – 5 sec]

Breathe into that awareness.

And with love, say silently:

"Thank you for keeping me safe. But I am ready to release."

[Pause – 5 sec]

Now, imagine that you are carrying a backpack. It feels heavy.

You've been carrying it for a long time.

Inside it are emotions, thoughts, and habits that no longer serve you.

[Pause—6sec]

 Feel the weight of that backpack.

Name what's inside: guilt... pain... loneliness... fear... Whatever it is for you.

[Pause – 5 sec]

Now gently... Take the backpack off. Feel how your shoulders relax.

How your breath deepens. How your body feels lighter.

You are not abandoning your story—you are setting it free.

[Pause—6sec]

Visualize yourself walking forward... lighter, freer, more alive.

See your body vibrant.

See your eyes clear.

See yourself smiling with love and pride.

[Pause – 5 sec]

Now repeat softly in your mind or aloud:

"I choose to care for myself."

"I nourish my body with love and awareness."

"I release what no longer serves me."

"I deserve to feel light—in body and soul."

[Pause—6sec]

Place your hand gently over your heart. Feel your breath... feel your presence... feel your power.

[Pause – 5 sec]

Every breath is a new beginning.

Every choice is a return to yourself.

You are free to choose differently, starting now.

[Pause—4sec]

You are not broken.

You are healing.

And the weight is not your identity—it's a message.

And now that you've listened… you can let it go.

[Pause—6sec]

Thank you… for honoring yourself today. Keep breathing.

Keep trusting.

Your freedom has already begun.

[**Music slowly fades out**.]

CHAPTER 17

FREEING YOU FROM PHOBIAS

When Fear Has Invisible Roots

For years, I had an uncontrollable fear of water. Swimming pools, the sea, or any place where the water was deep would trigger extreme anxiety in me. No one understood why—not even I did. It limited me, embarrassed me, and made me avoid situations that others found enjoyable.

It wasn't until I experienced a regression that I discovered the root of that fear: at the age of seven, my father took me to a swimming pool under the pretense of teaching me how to swim. Instead of protecting me, he took me to the deepest part... and raped me.

It was such a traumatic event that my mind, in an attempt to protect me, blocked it out completely. But the body never forgets. Nothing truly disappears—it only transforms into symptoms, illnesses, or phobias.

For years, my kidneys were affected, and my fear of water became increasingly intense. I couldn't understand the connection until that repressed memory surfaced. It was painful, yes—but it was also the beginning of my liberation.

Today, I know that many phobias are not absurd or exaggerated: they are cries from the unconscious—signals from a wound that longs to be recognized.

Through **regression hypnosis** and therapeutic work, it is possible to find the root of fear, embrace the wounded part within, and begin a profound healing process.

Freeing yourself from a phobia is not just about no longer feeling afraid—it's about recovering a part of yourself that got trapped in the past.

What Is a Phobia?

A phobia is an intense and disproportionate fear of something that, in appearance, poses no real threat. We often believe it's something irrational or senseless, but in reality, behind a phobia, there is usually an **untold story**.

Phobias are messages from the unconscious. They speak to us about something we haven't wanted—or been able—to face. A traumatic memory, a repressed emotion, a forgotten experience... All of it remains stored in the deeper mind and often shows up as **fear**.

Fears That Protect

Some fears serve as protection. A fear of flying might be covering a deeper fear of loss or losing control. Fear of public speaking may be rooted in humiliation or rejection.

Even fears of animals, heights, or enclosed spaces may come from a specific moment in your story—even if you no longer consciously remember it.

The unconscious is wise. It speaks through symbols, sensations, dreams, and irrational reactions.

Instead of fighting your fear, you can learn to **listen** to it. To decode its message and bring light to what once remained in the shadows.

The Power of the Unconscious

Your unconscious mind holds every experience you've ever lived through, even the ones you don't consciously remember. It's like a silent library that stores everything: images, emotions, sounds, and sensations.

When something was too painful or traumatic, your mind may have blocked it to protect you. But that energy doesn't disappear— it transforms. And sometimes, it takes the shape of a **phobia**.

Freeing yourself from a phobia means allowing your unconscious to speak, to be heard, and to heal. And for that, there are powerful tools such as **hypnosis, guided visualization, conscious forgiveness**, and **emotional work**.

My Path to Liberation

When I discovered the origin of my phobia, I cried. I felt rage, fear, sadness, guilt… but also relief. Finally, I understood why I had felt that way for so long.

Through hypnosis, I was able to go back to that seven-year-old girl, to embrace her, to tell her she wasn't alone. And I began to set her free.

I worked on forgiveness—not to justify, but to **release myself from the burden**. I retrained my mind so that water would no longer represent danger but instead... cleansing, flow, and life.

Today, not only have my kidneys healed, but also I can be near water without fear; sometimes I even immerse myself in it as a symbol of transformation. I reclaimed what had been taken from me: my power, my trust, and my body.

How to Begin Healing a Phobia

Healing begins with **compassion**, not force. Trying to "overcome" a phobia by pushing through it often intensifies the fear.

Here are some therapeutic tools I use in my practice:

- **Regression hypnosis**: to access the original wound and bring healing to the root
- **Breathing and grounding techniques**: to calm the nervous system when fear arises
- **Gradual desensitization**: gently exposing yourself to what you fear, step by step
- **Inner child work**: offering care and safety to the

younger self that still feels threatened

• **Affirmations and visualization**: to rewire the mind and restore inner safety

Healing Exercises to Free Yourself from Phobias
1. Dialogue with Your Fear
- Sit in a quiet, peaceful place.
- Take a deep breath.
- Close your eyes and visualize your fear as if it were a character or figure.
- Ask it: *"What are you trying to tell me?"*
- Listen without judgment.
- Write it down afterwards. What emerges may surprise you.

2. Returning to the Origin (Guided Visualization)

- Lie down somewhere comfortable.
- Breathe slowly and deeply for 3 minutes.
- Imagine yourself walking down a staircase with ten steps.
- On the last step, ask your mind to show you when that fear first began.
- Trust whatever comes—even if it feels strange or

painful.

- Visualize yourself entering the scene as your adult self.
- Embrace your younger self. Say what she needed to hear.
- When you're ready, climb the stairs and return to the present.
- Give thanks. Rest.

Note: This exercise can be very emotional. If you experience intense feelings, seek therapeutic support. You are not alone.

3. Positive Reprogramming

- Write a phrase that transforms your fear into personal power. Examples:
  - *"I am free and safe in contact with water."*
  - *"My body and mind are at peace."*
- Repeat this affirmation every morning and every night with your hand over your heart.

4. Safety Anchor

- Choose an image, scent, or sound that makes you feel safe.
- Whenever fear arises, use it to remind your mind that **you are safe now**.

- Over time, your nervous system will begin to rewire itself.

Audio Tool for Healing Phobias

Guided self-hypnosis or deep meditation audio can be a powerful tool for phobia healing—especially when it allows access to the unconscious with **safety and tenderness**.

Here is a suggested script and structure for a therapeutic audio, which you can record with your own warm and soothing voice.

"Embrace Your Fear: Healing Phobia from the Soul"
Recommended Length:

20–25 minutes

Suggested Background Music:

- Soft instrumental (piano, Tibetan bowls, nature sounds)
- Binaural tones or healing frequencies like 528 Hz (emotional healing) or 432 Hz (inner harmony)

Audio Script – Self-Hypnosis to Release a Phobia

(Soft, calming tone)

Welcome to this self-hypnosis session.

This is a space for you—where you can feel calm, protected,

and safe.

Settle into a quiet place.

Close your eyes... and begin to connect with your breath. Inhale deeply through your nose... and exhale slowly through your mouth.

Very good.

Do it two more times... And with each exhale, feel your body beginning to relax. That's it...

Now imagine in front of you a staircase.

It has ten steps, and each one takes you deeper into relaxation and connection with yourself.

As I count down from 10 to 1, you'll go down each step slowly... And with each number, you'll feel more at peace, more relaxed, and more at ease.

10...

9... slowly descending...

8... your mind softens...

7... your body loosens more and more...

6...

5... going deeper...

4... feeling calm...

3... almost there...

2... safe...

1... completely relaxed.

In front of you, there is a door.

This door leads to a memory—to the root of the fear you carry.

You are not alone.

Your adult self is with you—strong, wise, and loving.

When you open the door, you will simply **observe**.

You are not reliving it—you're witnessing it with compassion.

Open the door… and let your mind guide you. Observe… trust what arises.

What do you see? Where are you? How old are you?

Now, enter the scene as your adult self.

Approach your inner child… Look at her with love. Say to her:

"I'm here with you. You are not alone. This was not your fault. You are worthy, strong, and deeply loved."

Hug her.

Protect her.

Stay with her until she feels calm—until she feels safe with you.

[Pause]

Now visualize a scene in which you are free from this fear.

You see yourself strong, confident, and at peace.

You are in that place that once frightened you… And now you enjoy it.

You smile. You breathe calmly.

Listen to the new affirmation inside you:

"My mind and body are safe. I am free from fear. I trust myself."

Repeat it mentally…

Feel it as a deep truth that rises from within.

[Pause]

It's time to return. Thank your inner child.

Thank your unconscious mind for allowing this journey of healing.

Now imagine yourself climbing back up the ten steps…

Each step gently brings you back to the present…

1…

2…

3… returning with calm…

4… with renewed energy…

5…

6…

7… a soft smile on your face…

8…

9… moving your hands slowly…

10… opening your eyes gently…

You are back.

Take a deep breath.

You are safe.

You are alive.

You are healing.

Guided Visualization: Meeting Your Fear

Close your eyes and take a deep breath.

Imagine that your fear appears in front of you in the form of a figure.

It may look strange, small, or powerful.

But it's not here to harm you—it's here to deliver a message.

What does it look like?

How does it move?

How does it feel?

Now step closer to it with compassion. Ask gently:

"What are you trying to protect me from?"

And listen.

Maybe you feel an emotion rise. That's okay.

Let it move through you.

Now imagine holding the hand of that fearful part of yourself… and whisper:

"I see you. I'm here now. You are safe with me."

Affirmations for Inner Safety

Repeat these slowly, in your mind or aloud:

- "I am not my fear—I am greater than it."
- "My body is safe. My mind is healing."
- "I listen to the part of me that was once afraid."
- "I am reclaiming my freedom, step by step."
- "I am home. I am whole. I am free."

Final Reflection

Healing a phobia is not about pretending to be brave. It's about choosing to be **real**.

It's about walking inward, listening to the wounded voice within, and giving it what it never received: **presence, compassion, and care.**

*When you bring light to what was once hidden, fear begins to dissolve—and your **true self** begins to emerge.*

CHAPTER 18

CHANGING NEGATIVE THOUGHTS

When Your Mind Becomes Your Worst Enemy

Have you ever felt like your mind won't leave you alone?

As much as you try to move forward, an inner voice keeps reminding you of your mistakes, your fears, your "I can't" ... I've been there too. And I discovered something powerful: **We are not our thoughts.**

Negative thoughts are like gray clouds covering the sun. But the sun is always there, waiting for you to clear the sky.

Where Do Negative Thoughts Come From?

• Learned in childhood: criticism, demands, comparisons.

• Repeated over the years: automatic phrases like *"I'm not enough"* or *"This is going to go wrong."*

• Reinforced by unhealed emotions: guilt, fear, sadness.

The important thing to understand is this:

A thought is not a fact. It's just an interpretation. And we can change it.

My Personal Experience

There was a time when my mind was a constant source of judgment. It would tell me things like:

- "You're not good at this."
- "You'll always fail."
- "Who are you to even try?"

Those phrases didn't come from me...

They came from voices of the past that got trapped in my mind.

When I began to identify them, challenge them, and replace them — my life changed. It didn't happen overnight, but each transformed thought was a step closer to my inner paradise.

How to Change Negative Thoughts

1. Become Aware

- Write down the thoughts that repeat most often.
- Listen to what you think and say.
- Ask yourself: *Is this really true? Or just a belief?*
- Whose voice does it resemble?

2. Deactivate the Belief

• Change the question:

Instead of *"Why is this happening to me?"*, ask *"What purpose does this thought serve?"*

• Use humor or exaggeration to break the cycle:

If you think *"Everything will go wrong,"* imagine a dramatic parrot shouting it repeatedly. It takes away the power.

3. Reprogram with Empowering Affirmations

Examples:

• "I have the right to make mistakes and still be worthy."

• "My mind is learning to focus on the good."

• "I am stronger than my thoughts."

Practical Exercise: The Mental Switch

1. Close your eyes and visualize a light switch in your mind.

2. Every time you notice a negative thought, imagine switching it **off**.

3. Take a deep breath.

4. Turn **on** another switch: the one of calm, self-love, or trust.

5. Repeat a positive affirmation quietly or mentally.

Inspirational Quote for This Chapter

"Thoughts are like seeds. You choose which ones you water—and which ones you let dry."

Guided Meditation: Turning Negative Thoughts into Inner Light

Suggested duration: 10–15 minutes

Voice style: Soft, slow, warm

Background music: Gentle tones with natural sounds (water, wind, bowls)

You can find royalty-free music here:

- **YouTube Channels:**
  - Nu Meditation Music o
  - Meditative Mind
  - Yellow Brick Cinema *(always check license if publishing)*
- **Free Music Archive**

https://freemusicarchive.org/

Categories: "Ambient," "Instrumental," "Meditation"

- **Pixabay Music**

https://pixabay.com/music/

- **AudioJungle or Epidemic Sound** (paid, high-quality options)

Spoken Script – Meditation

Close your eyes.

Find a comfortable position. This is your moment… to let go of thoughts that don't belong to you and reconnect with your essence.

Take a deep breath…

And as you exhale, feel part of your body soften… Breathe again… and release tension,

pressure, doubt…

Now imagine you're sitting outside… In a peaceful place… surrounded by trees, or perhaps on the top of a quiet hill…

In front of you, there's a wide, infinite sky… Look up…

Notice how some dark clouds appear… Each

cloud represents a negative thought.

Maybe one says, "I'm *not enough.*"

Another might say, "I *always mess things up.*"

Don't fight them.

Just observe.

Those thoughts are not you.

They're just clouds.

And clouds—like thoughts—pass.

Now visualize a gentle breeze beginning to move those clouds... And behind them... the sun appears.

A warm, golden sun that was always there. That sun... is **you**.

It is your essence, your wisdom, your peace.

Feel the rays of that sun reaching your heart.

And from your heart, a soft light begins to expand...

A light that fills your mind and dissolves every thought of fear or judgment.

Repeat silently within you:

"I am not my thoughts.

I am the awareness that observes them.

I choose thoughts of love, trust, and truth."

Breathe deeply...

Stay in that light for a few moments...

feeling calm, clear, and free.

[Long pause]

When you're ready... Gently move your fingers...

Return to the present moment... Open your eyes...

And carry this peace, this light, this new perspective with you.

"Even the darkest night will end, and the sun will rise."

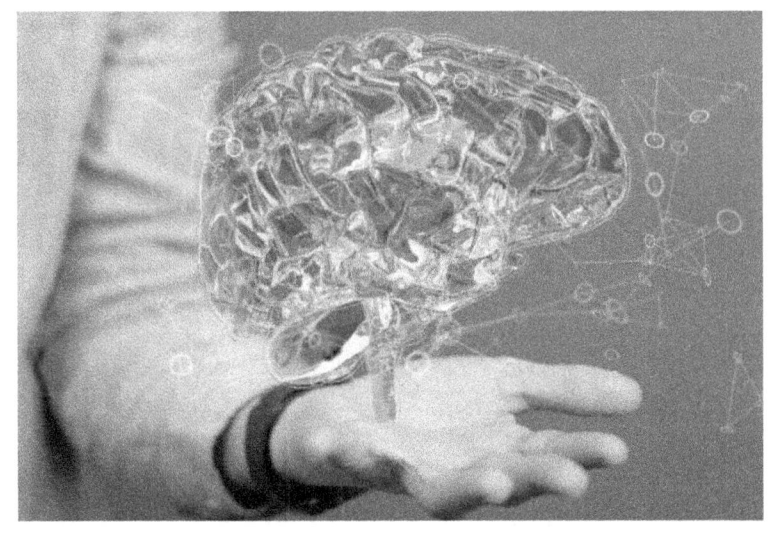

CHAPTER 19

HOW TO IMPROVE YOUR MEMORY

Memory Is a Garden

Memory is not a box where information is stored—it's a garden that needs care, attention, and light. Throughout life, many people feel like they "don't remember like they used to," that important things slip their minds, or that their mind feels foggy. But here's the good news: memory can be trained, nourished, and allowed to bloom.

Why Does Memory Weaken?

There are many possible reasons:

- Chronic stress or anxiety
- Lack of restful sleep
- Information overload (too much to remember without structure)
- Lack of mindfulness (living on autopilot)
- Unprocessed emotions (guilt, pain, past traumas)

The mind doesn't retain what it doesn't experience with awareness. That's why improving memory begins by living more **presently**.

My Personal Experience

There was a stage in my life when I felt like I was forgetting names, appointments—even what I had walked into a room for. I thought it was age or stress. But I discovered that, In truth, my mind was **overloaded**, **tired**, and **scattered**.

Through mindfulness exercises, breathing, visualization techniques, and small changes in my daily routine, I not only improved my memory... I also enhanced my **clarity**, **focus**, and **confidence**.

Exercises to Activate and Strengthen Your Memory

1. Attention Is Everything

What you don't pay attention to, you won't remember.

• Take conscious pauses. When someone tells you their name, look into their eyes and mentally repeat it.

• Observe with intention: What are they wearing? How do they move? What tone of voice do they use?

• When you live each moment with more presence, your natural memory awakens.

2. Visualize to Remember

•   Create mental images for what you want to remember. Example: If you meet someone named Rose, imagine a blooming rose above their head.

•   The more absurd or creative the image, the easier it is to recall.

3. Make Mental Lists with Emotion

•   When writing a shopping list or daily tasks, assign each item an emotion, a color, or an image.

•   The brain remembers what moves it emotionally.

4. Meditation for Connection

Memory lives in **calm**, not in noise.

•   Close your eyes, breathe deeply, and visualize your brain as a still lake.

•   Imagine information floating gently on the surface.

•   This state of relaxation helps your hippocampus—the brain's memory center—work more effectively.

5. Activate with Curiosity

•   Learn something new every day: a word, a recipe, or a fun fact. Curiosity strengthens neural connections.

•   Teach what you learn. Teaching is one of the best ways to remember.

Practical Tips

- **Sleep well**: Deep sleep consolidates memory.
- **Stay hydrated**: The brain needs water to function properly.
- **Move**: Walking activates the brain more than sitting still.
- **Write by hand**: Handwriting stimulates different brain areas that enhance memory.
- **Avoid multitasking**: Focusing on one thing at a time improves retention.

"Remembering is not just a mental function—it's an act of love for your story, your present, and your life."

Guided Meditation: Activate Your Memory with Light and Presence

Suggested duration: 10–12 minutes

Background music: Gentle instrumental (harp, Tibetan bowls, or soft piano)

Spoken Script – Meditation

Sit or lie down in a peaceful place.

Close your eyes.

This is your moment to connect with your inner clarity... and awaken your natural memory.

Take a deep breath...

Inhale through your nose…

Exhale through your mouth…

Do it three times…

And with each breath, feel your mind relax… your body let go…

Now, visualize your brain as a garden.

A garden full of paths, flowers, and glowing roots.

Each memory is a flower…

Each idea, a seed…

And you are the one who waters it, cares for it, and brings it light.

Now imagine a gentle light descending from the sky. A warm, golden light entering the top of your head… and beginning to illuminate your mind.

This light clears away fog… Dissolves stress…

And activates the connections between your thoughts.

Feel how this light travels through every corner of your brain… Lighting up your attention…

Activating your comprehension… Nourishing your ability to remember.

Repeat silently:

"My memory is alive and clear. I am present. I remember with ease and confidence."

Now imagine walking through your mental garden. You see the flowers of your memories… the leaves of your knowledge… and new buds beginning to grow.

Everything is in order.

Everything is blooming.

Stay here a few more seconds, breathing softly…

[Long pause]

Now, gently return…

Move your hands…

Your feet…

Stretch if you'd like…

And when you're ready, open your eyes… Your mind is clearer. Your memory, more awake.

Your attention is more present.

CHAPTER 20

HEALING THE RELATIONSHIP WITH ALCOHOL

You are not broken. You are seeking comfort.

For many people, alcohol is not just a drink. It's an escape, a momentary relief, a pressure valve when life feels too heavy. It may arrive with a social smile—a glass to relax, a celebration toast—but behind that ritual often lies a silent cry: the desire to disconnect from pain, emptiness, or emotional exhaustion.

I've seen that hidden cry many times. In clinical hypnosis sessions, I've accompanied people who didn't know how to say "enough," because alcohol had become an invisible companion. They weren't bad people. They weren't weak. They were simply trapped in a cycle they no longer knew how to break.

So today, I say to you: **You're not alone. Your freedom is not lost—it's just waiting for you to claim it.**

Andrés' Story: When the Body Says What the Soul Keeps Quiet

I remember Andrés (name changed), a 48-year-old man who came to my office utterly exhausted. Not from work, not from his family, but from the war within himself. He had quit alcohol more than once—and always returned. During our first session, his voice trembled:

"I don't want to lose everything," he said, **"but I feel like I can't do this anymore."**

Under hypnosis, Andrés relived a moment from childhood: hiding under a table while his parents fought. Frozen by fear. The little boy he once was couldn't understand why no one hugged him, why there was so much yelling. That wound stayed alive—hidden beneath layers of years... and alcohol.

When he was able to embrace that child within him with compassion, something shifted. He began to understand that his drinking wasn't a curse but a learned coping mechanism. It wasn't just about quitting alcohol—it was about **healing the pain that made him drink**.

Beyond Judgment: Understanding with Compassion

The relationship with alcohol is not just physical. It has **emotional**, **mental**, and even **spiritual** roots. Many people who struggled with this addiction once didn't know how to ease their anxiety, sadness, or loneliness any other way. Using alcohol to "relax" is not weakness—it's a failed attempt at emotional self-regulation. But what once helped you survive... no longer helps you live fully.

This chapter is not a sermon, nor a list of prohibitions. It's an **invitation to** look at yourself with tenderness, to acknowledge your wounds without shame, and to reclaim your power of choice.

Exercise to Reconnect with Yourself

1. Emotional Awareness Journal

For one week, write down every time you feel the urge to drink:

- What emotion are you feeling at that moment?
- What happened right before the urge?
- What part of you is seeking comfort?

Observing without judgment is the first step toward freedom.

2. Replace the Ritual

If alcohol has become a ritual (e.g., after work or during social gatherings), create a new one:

- Calming tea + soft music
- Mindful walk
- Deep breathing with positive affirmations
- Journaling: *"Today I choose to care for myself."*

Make self-care your new habit.

3. Guided Visualization: Meeting Your Free Self Close your eyes. Breathe deeply.

Imagine walking down a path of light.

At the end, you meet a version of yourself—free from alcohol. Observe your skin, your eyes, and your energy.

Ask this "you": *What did you do to heal?*

Listen. Thank them. Embrace them.

Repeat this daily to strengthen your purpose.

Liberating Affirmations

• "Each day I choose consciously. My soul breathes more freely."

• "I am not defined by what I consumed, but by who I choose to become today."

• "My past doesn't bind me. My present empowers me."

• "Saying 'no' to alcohol is saying 'yes' to life."

Closing: Returning to Yourself

Alcohol doesn't have to be your enemy.

It's simply a signal—that something inside you needs **more love**, more **attention**, and more **truth**.

Don't fight yourself. Instead, embrace your story. See yourself. And take just one step toward your freedom.

And if tomorrow you stumble—it's okay. Your strength lies not in never falling, but in rising with **more compassion than judgment**.

You can do this.

Your inner paradise is closer than you think.

And when you find it, you'll no longer need anything to numb yourself—because *you'll be awake. Present. Alive. Free.*

Self-Hypnosis Audio: Healing the Relationship with Alcohol Recording Instructions:

- Duration: 15–20 minutes
- Background Music: Soft instrumental (no vocals), nature sounds, or frequencies like 432 Hz or 528 Hz

Suggested Tracks:

- *528 Hz Positive Transformation & Healing*
- *Inner Peace – Calm Meditation Music with Water Sounds*

Important:

Keep the music subtle—like a whisper beneath your voice. Leave silent spaces for key pauses and inner reflection.

Self-Hypnosis Script:

(Use a warm, calm voice) I close my eyes slowly…

Take a deep breath through my nose… And exhale gently through my mouth… That's it… Very good.

With every breath, my body begins to relax... My feet unwind... my legs... my hips...

Each exhale takes me deeper...

As if descending a gentle staircase...

10... going deeper...

9... more and more relaxed...

8... my mind quiets...

7... releasing all tension...

6... feeling lighter...

5... even more calm...

4... beautiful...

3... safe and steady...

2... almost there...

1... completely relaxed...

Now, in this deep state of calm...

I imagine a new version of myself in front of me... A version that has already healed from alcohol...

My gaze is clear, my skin radiant, and my energy peaceful and strong. That version is me—but more free, more conscious, more me.

Alcohol no longer has power over me. I have taken back control of my life.

Because I am stronger than any substance.

I imagine a moment when I feel the urge to drink... I place

that urge in my hands.

I look at it closely. I recognize it was just an attempt to ease pain, to fill a void…

I thank it—and then I let it go.

I watch it float away with the wind… And I feel deep relief as it disappears.

I repeat:

"I choose freedom."

"My body is a temple."

"Each day, I grow stronger and more conscious."

 I no longer need alcohol to relax, to escape, or to belong. I can now do all that—from my true self.

I breathe in freedom, peace, and self-love.

And with each day, my desire for alcohol fades more and more… While my desire to take care of myself—to heal and live with clarity—grows.

I can say no.

And that "no" is a YES to myself.

To my life.

To my well-being.

To the people I love.

To the version of me who came here to shine.

Every cell in my body celebrates this decision. My liver, my lungs, and my heart—all thank me. My mind clears.

My spirit lifts.

I am free.

I have found my paradise.

Soon I will return to the present moment… Bringing with me this strength and freedom.

I'll count from 1 to 5, and when I reach 5, I will open my eyes—renewed.

1… gently moving my fingers…

2… breathing deeper…

3… feeling light and energized…

4… bringing back all this transformation…

5… opening my eyes… Welcome back.

Final tip: Listen to the audio several times, especially when you feel like drinking. Each time, strengthen your release more.

I am free. I am me.

CHAPTER 21

ACT AS IF YOU HAD ALREADY FOUND PARADISE

The mind doesn't distinguish between what's real and what's vividly imagined.

When you act as if everything is working out, your mind starts creating that reality as if it were law. **Anything the mind can conceive and believe can be achieved.** It depends on your inner conviction. When you act as if everything is going well, something unlocks. You become a magnet that transforms every circumstance.

Do you want to succeed? Then act as if you already have:
- Dress like a successful person.
- Think like one.
- Make decisions from the certainty of success.
- Speak to yourself as the powerful being you truly are.

Because when you embody that version with conviction, your internal vibration changes… and that changes everything you attract.

Acting "as if" doesn't mean ignoring obstacles.

It means facing them with the certainty that on the other side, victory awaits. It means understanding that opportunities often come disguised, and your determination must be stronger than your excuses.

You don't need proof to believe.

You need to believe so that proof can appear.

Because the universe doesn't respond to your doubts, it responds to your conviction. When you act as if you're already successful, you stop surrounding yourself with mediocrity.

You let go of negative thoughts that once seemed normal.

Most people don't fail from a lack of talent but **from not aligning what they think, feel, say, and do.** They act from fear, from insecurity.

But you've already decided to live each day, all day, as if everything is aligned. And to act accordingly. If your thoughts are positive but your actions are weak, you're sending mixed signals. **Choose coherence.**

- Think as if you're unstoppable.
- Speak as if you already have it.
- Act as if everything is happening for you.

That coherence builds synchronicity:

- The right people show up.

- The exact opportunities appear.
- Unexpected solutions manifest.

Successful people don't have easier lives. They have stronger expectations.

And those expectations are like magnets. They attract ideas, allies, and results that others call luck.

But it's not luck; it's synchronicity. Not coincidence, but conviction. Not chance, but attitude.

Those who walk toward the top, believing the path will open, see doors where others see walls, see bridges where others see cliffs, and see opportunities where others only see problems.

One of the invisible enemies of success is indecision—saying "I'll try" instead of "I'll achieve it."

Make a pact with yourself:
- A pact of power.
- A pact of faith.
- A pact with your destiny.

Because everything you're hoping for…**is also hoping for you.** Have you ever noticed how some people enter a room and instantly command attention?

It's not their clothes. It's not their appearance. **It's their energy.**

That high vibration, that air of certainty, that calm strength, that quiet determination. That's the **frequency of success**.

How do you see yourself when no one is watching? That's where your true power begins. Not with what you have, but with what you're able to imagine with conviction.

Act as if you already are who you want to be. Feel as if you already have what you desire. And the world will have to catch up with you.

This principle is law.

When you imagine vividly, you act differently. You speak differently. You walk differently.

You project a frequency that transforms your surroundings, because you're no longer acting from lack—but from certainty.

This isn't about daydreaming. It's about living the outcome inside **yourself** before it shows up on the outside. And that changes everything.

Do you want an abundant bank account?
Imagine how it feels to know money flows with ease.
Do you want freedom of time?
Visualize yourself as the owner of your days, not a slave to the clock.

Do you want extraordinary relationships?

Love yourself. Respect yourself. Walk like someone who already feels complete, loved, and at peace.

Because that paradise you were searching for outside…**begins when you choose to live it from within.**

CLOSING MESSAGE

Thank you for walking this path with me. This book is not only the story of how I found my paradise but also a loving invitation for you to find yours, too.

It doesn't matter where you start; what truly transforms your life is where you choose to go from here.

If you've reached this point, you've already taken a huge step: you've awakened. You've begun to look at yourself with more love, more compassion, and more power.

This is not the end—**it's the rebirth** of a new version of you: more conscious, freer, more you.

Always remember: your mind is a wonderful tool, and your heart is the bridge to everything you dream of.

You have permission to shine.
To heal.
To change.
To make mistakes and try again. You have permission to be happy.

And most of all, **you have the ability to create a life that feels like home.**

We'll meet again on every page you reread, in every exercise you practice, and in every moment when you choose to act as if you already are that extraordinary person you've always been.

With love and deep gratitude, **Myriam Grajales**

MESSAGE TO THE READER

To you, who dared to look within.

To you, who searched for answers and found strength.

To you, who once doubted your worth and now recognize yourself as light.

I dedicate this book to your silent courage, to your longing to heal, and to that inner fire that refuses to go out.

Thank you for allowing me to walk with you. Thank you for existing.

Thank you for choosing yourself.

Because paradise is not a place… It's a state of consciousness.
And now that you've found it within you, the whole world will begin to reflect it.

TESTIMONIALS FROM THERAPIES WITH MYRIAM GRAJALES

Mrs. Sherman

Dear Myriam,

You have helped me more than I could ever imagine.

You are an angel from heaven.

You freed me from pain.

I love you.

Jaime Montoya

Before meeting Myriam, I was someone who got angry at everything.

I lived stressed and grumpy.

Thanks to her therapies, I experienced a complete transformation. Now I enjoy each day without wasting it in anger, and I live my life with calm.

A thousand thanks!

Diana Perdomo

When I met Myriam, she noticed my fears and insecurities and helped me realize they were a problem.

I thought it was normal, something that couldn't be changed… But with her help, I understood that I could heal.

Myriam helped me overcome many traumas, to stop the overwhelming pace of my life, and to start enjoying each day.

Today, I have my own business, I'm confident in myself, and the most beautiful part is now I can also help others.

I'm deeply grateful for her belief in me and for her constant support and dedication.

You are a wonderful woman.

Mikael Theoktisto (Düsseldorf, Germany – June 10, 2025) I met Myriam in an unexpected way, while waiting for my connecting flight in Panama. That day we spoke about the mind and how hypnosis can help a person change their reality.

Soon it was time to board. We exchanged contacts, and before leaving, she told me, "If you ever need help, write to me."

Almost a year went by. One day, in the midst of deep sadness and not knowing who to turn to, I remembered Myriam. I reached out, and we scheduled our first session. I told her about my struggles… and she immediately began to help me.

Since then, she has been a guide for me. She has helped me feel better about myself, face my fears, and love myself more each day.

Today I know that the way we speak to ourselves can truly transform our lives. One day you wake up, smile... and start seeing wonders everywhere.

Thank you, Myriam. Please keep helping others. The world needs you.

Yolanda Giraldo

My name is Yolanda, and I wholeheartedly recommend Myriam Grajales as an exceptional therapist. She helped me love myself and develop true self-love.

Because of my past, I was a woman full of insecurities; I didn't love myself, and I lived with deep depression. But thanks to Myriam, today I'm a different person, confident, empowered, and with strong self-esteem. I'm a triumphant woman now.

Thank you so much, Myriam, for teaching me how to love myself.

Josseline C.

I never imagined how powerful hypnotherapy could be until I experienced it myself. For years, I carried anxiety and depression that held me back. After just a few sessions, I felt lighter, more at peace, and more in control of my life than ever before. It was as if a heavy burden I didn't even know I was carrying had finally been lifted.

Hypnotherapy has truly changed my life. And Myriam saved it.

Fanny Echeverri

In 2009, I began experiencing intense pain in my spine, specifically in the lumbar vertebrae L4 and L5 and the cervical vertebrae C4 and C5. It was a time of deep physical and emotional suffering. The pain was so strong that I was sometimes incapacitated for entire weeks, unable to stay in the same position for more than 15 minutes. I lived with constant limitations, and every movement was a challenge.

Doctors gave me two options: spinal surgery or epidural steroid injections, which I received about every six months, depending on how much pain I could bear. Surgery seemed inevitable.

But in 2014, I was blessed to begin therapy with Myriam Grajales. It was a turning point in my life. Through her guidance, I began exploring the emotional root of my pain—something I had thought impossible, especially since X-rays showed irreversible damage in my spine.

Myriam's sessions helped me uncover and release deep emotions, many of which had been hidden in my unconscious mind for self-protection. With each session, I felt a weight lift, and my body began to heal.

The results were astonishing: not only did I cancel the surgery, But—miraculously and to the glory of God—I have never felt that spinal pain again. Today, June 5, 2025, I remain completely pain-free, and my body feels strong.

I also learned that when we remember what our unconscious mind has hidden, we set ourselves free. We see life with greater clarity, and we open ourselves to forgiveness—especially toward ourselves.

I share this because I have medical proof of the physical transformation, but the inner transformations—subtle yet deeply powerful—have marked a before and after in my life.

To Myriam, my deepest respect and heartfelt gratitude for your love, your time, and your wisdom. May God continue to use you as an instrument of healing for many more lives, as you have been for mine.

Rafael González

I used to ride only a bicycle because I was terrified of traveling by motorcycle, car, bus—or even worse, a plane. I missed out on family trips with my wife and children. I would arrive at work sweaty from riding my bike.

A friend recommended that I seek help from Myriam Grajales. It was total liberation. Through several regression sessions, we explored the root of each trauma.

Today, I enjoy traveling and making up for lost time. Thank you, Myriam, for setting me free.

Julieta Perdomo

"I had an unexplainable phobia of water—whether it was a pool or the ocean. I sought help from Myriam Grajales, and thanks to her therapy, I was able to reach the origin of that fear—something I didn't even remember, because it was so traumatic.

When I was five years old, I went to the beach with my family. I was playing near the shore when a wave pulled me out into the sea. No one noticed. I thought I was going to die... until something—I'm not sure what—pushed me back to the shore. My family remained distracted, unaware of what I had just experienced.

After healing with Myriam, I took swimming lessons, tried surfing, and even water skiing. I returned to the water without fear.

Myriam's therapy is truly powerful."

BIOGRAPHY

Myriam In How I Found My Paradise, and You Can Too, she shares not only her professional experience but also personal experiences, reflections, and practical exercises that have transformed her life and the lives of those she has accompanied in consultation.

Myriam Grajales has been a clinical hypnotherapist since 1995, with a career dedicated to accompanying hundreds of people on their path to emotional healing, self-love, and personal transformation.

Her passion is to help others discover that well-being and happiness are not distant goals but rather states that are built day by day from within.

With a warm, close, and deep human style, she combines tools of clinical hypnosis, personal development, positive psychology, and practical spirituality to guide her readers towards a fuller, freer, and more conscious life.

Her passion is to help others discover that well-being and happiness are not distant goals but rather states that are built day by day from within.

In How I Found My Paradise, and You Can Too, she shares not only her professional experience but also personal experiences, reflections, and practical exercises that have transformed her life and the lives of those she has accompanied in consultation.

Her mission is simple but powerful: to remind you that you have the power to Create your own paradise, here and now.

www.myriamgrajales.com

www.ingramcontent.com/pod-product-compliance
Lightning Source LLC
Chambersburg PA
CBHW021156160426
43194CB00007B/768